C000102847

London Ghosts Unveiled

The True Stories behind the Capital's Hauntings

Karen & William Ellis-Rees

Copyright © Karen Ellis-Rees & William Ellis-Rees 2021

All rights reserved. This includes the right to reproduce
any portion of this book in any form.

ISBN: 979-8-366-40519-5

For Tom and Anna

Contents

Introduction

WHETHER OR NOT you believe in ghosts, you may be curious to know what really lies behind tales of the supernatural. These ten stories lift the lid on a clutch of London hauntings, with a cast of characters that includes a taphophobe, two fraudsters and a sulky teenager.

The Bermondsey Poltergeist

IN THE YEAR 1857 Sarah and Charles Bacon were terrified by strange happenings in their small house in London Street in Bermondsey. Who would have thought it? Bermondsey — modern Bermondsey — is a fashionable area of South East London. Bermondsey has gastropubs and street markets, quiet gardens and dedicated cycle routes. Bermondsey folk live in converted warehouses and cosy Victorian terraces. They stroll around galleries and enjoy convivial get-togethers in bars and restaurants built into old railway arches. Bermondsey is definitely a good place to be.

But back in the nineteenth century the Bacons may well have thought otherwise. For the Bermondsey they knew was an unhealthy sprawl of rickety buildings and menacing passageways, and very much a place where you might be kept awake at night by the sounds in the streets outside, where stray cats howled, and mad dogs barked, and drunken brawlers settled scores with their fists. But they were disturbed not by what was going on outside, but by the odd and eerie happenings that were, well, happening inside. Meanwhile Caroline, who was Charles's daughter, and Sarah's sullen and resentful stepdaughter, had her mind on other things. She was thirteen, and wanted to be out roaming the streets with her friends. Sadly, Sarah and Charles did not approve of Caroline's friends, or of young girls roaming the streets.

For five days mysterious noises had resounded at all hours throughout the building. When Charles was at work during the day — at the age of fifty-six, when he might have felt that he was entitled to a rest, he was still driving his cart along the cobbled roads and lanes of Bermondsey — things got even worse. Plates and bowls and glasses flew from shelves without warning and without cause, and smashed into pieces as they landed on the floor.

Sarah was acutely aware of a malevolent presence in the house, invisible and destructive. She was no longer young enough to be brave in the face of these alarming incidents. She was fifty-three, and attached to her possessions, and afraid that she was going to lose them all. Nor did Charles and Sarah have the slightest idea what the 'presence' would do next. Their one comfort at this unsettling time was that the flying crockery and glassware overshadowed the troubles they were having with Caroline. They almost felt like a family again.

Rumours of the haunting soon got about. The details were discussed by the huddled groups loitering on street corners. Theories were traded in doorways. Gross exaggerations of established facts were perpetrated in taverns, the stretching of the truth bearing a close relationship to the lateness of the hour and the consumption of drink. Men scoffed and expressed defiance in the face of the manifest evil. Women quietly prayed that they were not next in line for a visit from whatever was terrorising the Bacons. Children acted as if they were not interested, but secretly they were very afraid.

Evening after evening, night after night, large crowds gathered in the hope of seeing or hearing the ghost. Nor should we be surprised, for rubbernecking was a popular Victorian pastime. Crowds flocked to Newgate in 1857 to witness the last moments of Robert Thomas

Davis, who had murdered his wife in a fit of drunken jealousy. They lined the pavements of Regent Street, the Strand and Whitechapel to ogle Major Tom Thumb, pulled in his tiny toy carriage by Shetland ponies. They pushed and shoved their way into Lambeth Police Court, or stood outside in even greater numbers, hissing and booing when Martha Bacon — no relation — was taken in for questioning following the death of her two little children. They gathered to satisfy their morbid curiosity, certainly, but also to broaden their minds by listening to street musicians and street preachers.

For five or six nights the horde of curious onlookers grew not only in number but also in rowdiness. The occupants of nearby houses were very inconvenienced. The neighbourhood tradesmen and tradeswomen were very inconvenienced. The local public houses were not in the slightest inconvenienced. There were said to be over a thousand people gathering in the narrow streets and alleys. Tensions were rising and tempers fraying, and so on the nights of the 12th and 13th of November between twenty and thirty police constables, under the command of Superintendent Branford and Inspector Mackintosh, were mobilised to disperse the crowds and prevent an attack on the house of the Bacons.

This house was in just the right place for a haunting. For London Street, where the Bacons lived, was in the notorious Bermondsey 'rookery' known to one and all as Jacob's Island, which, while not an island in the strict sense of the word, was bordered in a watery way by the River Thames and St Saviour's Dock, by the River Neckinger, and by Hickman's Folly, which cut a swathe from east to west and was probably none too salubrious or safe. The interior of the 'island' was densely packed with ramshackle and crowded houses surrounded by filthy man-made ditches, which had been dug in the seventeenth century to provide a ready supply of water for the mills and the lead factories and the tanneries with their awful stench of urine and dog shit. Along these Stygian streams men would navigate gloomily in punts, dipping their poles into the oily waters as they passed beneath low wooden footbridges and beetling brick buildings begrimed with the filth of years beyond counting. They were figures in the worst sort of desolate urban landscape.

A clergyman by the name of Thomas Beames, who had seen for himself the horrifying living conditions in the worst corners of the metropolis, wrote down his observations in his book *The Rookeries of London*, which he published in 1852. According to Beames the houses of Jacob's Island

> are evidently old, the first storeys slightly overhanging the ground floor, yet not so much as in many of our old towns where these projections form penthouses: there is nothing particularly quaint and interesting about them; hovels they were, and hovels will they remain as long as they exist.

Until the late 1830s, when Charles Dickens wrote *Oliver Twist*, only those who had the misfortune to live there would have heard of Jacob's Island. Towards the end of the novel Bill Sikes travels down to Bermondsey to hide after the murder of his lover Nancy, and it is there that he meets his own end, accidentally hanging himself above Folly Ditch. Dickens's description in Chapter 50 of the setting for the odious criminal's death has the following disturbing passage:

> In Jacob's Island, the warehouses are roofless and empty; the walls are crumbling down; the windows are windows no more; the doors are falling into the streets; the chimneys are blackened, but they yield no

smoke. Thirty or forty years ago, before losses and chancery suits came upon it, it was a thriving place; but now it is a desolate island indeed. The houses have no owners; they are broken open, and entered upon by those who have the courage; and there they live, and there they die. They must have powerful motives for a secret residence, or be reduced to a destitute condition indeed, who seek a refuge in Jacob's Island.

Now, the Bacons had lived in the area for many years. Charles married his first wife, Rachel Ball, in 1827. They had at least seven children, of whom Caroline, who was born in about 1841, was the youngest. Several of the remaining six died in infancy, a not uncommon fate in that part of the metropolis. All too many of the residents were poor and underfed and drank water drawn from ditches full of industrial and human waste. In the summer of 1849, when London was in the grip of cholera, over half of its twelve-and-a-half thousand victims died south of the river. Bermondsey was one such transpontine area ravaged by the epidemic, and the journalist Henry Mayhew, who went there to investigate in person, made it the subject of a searing piece that he published in *The Morning Post*. He was clearly shocked by what he saw, and he described Jacob's Island as a 'loathsome place' that had not seen any changes, let alone improvements, since the time of the fire of London, by which, ironically, it was spared, being south of the Thames. The air was heavy with pestilential odours — 'the smell of a graveyard' — strong enough to make the uninitiated feel decidedly queasy. The water that oozed and slithered in a nastily viscous manner through the Island

is covered with a scum almost like a cobweb, and prismatic with grease. In it float large masses of green rotting weed and against the posts of the bridges are swollen carcasses of dead animals, almost bursting with the gases of putrefaction.

Mayhew was transfixed by the water. In full sunlight it had the colour of strong green tea, but elsewhere, in the shade, it was as black as marble. He listened to the gurgle of the drains and sewers as they added their own soupy contents to the creek. He saw white-limbed boys bathing in it as one would bathe in a mountain stream. And to his utter dismay he spotted a little girl leaning out from the window of a house, and lowering a tin can at the end of a rope into the slime below in order to fill a large bucket that stood at her side. Of course, Mayhew had no idea who she was. Perhaps — *perhaps* — she was Caroline Bacon at the age of eight or thereabouts.

Caroline's mother — Rachel — died in March 1852 at the age of forty-eight and was buried in the graveyard of St Mary Magdalen in Bermondsey Street. Within seven months Charles was married again, this time to a widow by the name of Sarah Tuckey. In an age when mourning was required by custom, this was a hasty move. But he might have been lonely. He might have needed the income of two working adults to survive. Or he might have wanted a mother for the two daughters who remained at home. But only a few years after Sarah joined the household, the disturbances started.

In those dark November days in 1857 a desperate Charles begged for help from the priest at the Roman Catholic church of the Most Holy Trinity, which stood at the top of Parker's Row. The Bacons were not Catholics, but it may be that someone had suggested to Charles that they needed an exorcism. The priest refused to intervene or have anything to do with the Bermondsey Ghost, whereupon the matter came to the notice of Mr

Hancock from the District Visiting Society, an organisation that encouraged the poor of the parish to attend church and Sunday school by giving them clothes and small handouts. Mr Hancock duly visited the house in London Street to investigate, and with him went the vicar of Christ Church in Parker's Row, the Reverend Martin. In this matter Hancock and Martin were a sort of ecclesiastical Holmes and Watson.

The good vicar, whose full name was Robert Marshall Martin, and who was a graduate of St Edmund Hall in Oxford, had been the curate of Christ Church from the time it was built in 1845. He lived in Bermondsey with his family, and he knew Charles Bacon as a good worker and Sarah Bacon as a respectable woman. But as soon as he questioned the family, he rejected outright the idea of a ghostly presence, as did Hancock. Being rational men, they were convinced that the perpetrator of the nuisance was to be found close to home, and they were probably the ones who persuaded Charles to bring his daughter before the magistrate at Southwark Police Court in Blackman Street in Borough.

There, on the afternoon of the 15th of November, Caroline was charged with wilful damage to her father's goods. The Reverend Martin declared that he knew the girl as an occasional scholar at the local ragged school, which failed her so spectacularly that even as an adult she was unable to write her name. In spite of his presumed belief in redemption he regarded her as bad, and idle, and beyond reforming. Meanwhile Charles told the magistrate that he was at his wits' end with a recalcitrant daughter who only ever wanted to be out on the streets, keeping bad company. Caroline in her turn announced petulantly that she had become the 'ghost' to punish her parents for not letting her join her friends. She was obviously not stupid, and explained how she had attached almost invisible strands of hair to cups and glasses in order to send the objects tumbling with a single tug when no one was looking. Her stepmother, who had been in the same room during most of these acts, was astonished at these seemingly supernatural happenings.

The magistrate, Mr Boyce Harvey Combe, did not take kindly to a girl who had scared her parents, destroyed their property, and diverted a large number of policemen from their legitimate business of preventing crime. There was little weight given to what today might be seen as mitigating factors — her youth, the loss of her mother and her young siblings, her father's hasty remarriage — so Combe sentenced Caroline to two weeks in the Wandsworth House of Correction in the hope that this would persuade her to mend her ways. But, as so often happens, punishment did not have the desired effect, and on her release Caroline returned home as disobedient as before. Unable to control his daughter, but unwilling to abandon her entirely, Charles had her admitted to a private reformatory. When she escaped, he sent her to another institution, which obligingly expelled her on the grounds that she was both incorrigible and uncontrollable.

Charles then persuaded another daughter, Rachel, who had recently married, to take Caroline in for a small weekly consideration. Even though Caroline stole a watch from the couple — she sold it and pocketed the money — Rachel and her husband Frederick Epps later allowed her back into their home. The last straw was the pawning of a bundle of clothes that Rachel, who worked as a washwoman, or at least took in mending, had instructed Caroline to return to a client. So it should come as no surprise that a 'Caroline Bacon' appears more than once in the records of workhouse casual wards. And she was in the workhouse in Rotherhithe when in July 1863, at the age of nineteen, she fetched up in court again. Something had upset the volatile girl, and she had promptly set about destroying the clothes she had been given at the workhouse. When it was put to her that she was from too good a family home to take up space and resources in the workhouse, she said, as she always did, that she could not live with her cruel stepmother. A police investigation proved that Caroline was lying about poor Sarah, and that even when her father provided her with alternative accommodation, *sans* her stepmother, she still ran away to lead a dissolute life on the streets. On hearing which the magistrate sentenced her to a month's imprisonment.

Where Caroline was thereafter is more or less a mystery. She makes a brief appearance in 1875 when she marries a John Thomas Cox in Bethnal Green, with her long-suffering brother-in-law Frederick Epps as a witness. But then she seems to vanish into thin air, to become invisible, just as the 'ghost' she had once been at the age of thirteen simply ceased to exist. Not that she was in any way unique. London has had its fair share of ghosts and poltergeists that have turned out to be resentful or unhappy adolescents, like Caroline. The Stockwell Ghost was a downtrodden young servant. The Cock Lane ghost was a girl cynically manipulated by her father. And in the twentieth century the Wycliff Road poltergeist was believed by some to be a fifteen-year-old who could make eerie knockings with her hammertoes.

The Peckham Ghost

ON SUNDAY THE 10th of November 1872, just before seven o'clock in the evening, Misses Constance and Margaret Carver were preparing to go to church. Constance was sixteen years old. Margaret was fifteen. With them was their governess, Mary Prentice, a young woman from Norfolk in her early twenties. All three lived in a suite of well-appointed rooms in the South Wing of Dulwich College, where the two girls' father, Canon Alfred Carver, was the Master.

Margaret was the first to the door, which she opened in order to step out on to the carriage drive. As she did so, she caught herself thinking how oddly dark it was outside. The nearest gas lamp, which stood opposite the door, was not lit. When lit it cast a comforting glow over the carriage drive, making the world of shadows and silhouettes less threatening, less unnerving, less a place fit only for the spirits of the dead. But now, without the light from the lamp, it was darker than dark.

What happened next happened in a matter of a second or two. Margaret was through the door, and, as she stepped outside, she noticed a shape moving in her direction. And although the gas lamp was not lit, and although it was darker than dark, Margaret saw that the shape was the figure of a man, tall of stature and horribly white from head to toe. The figure had its arms stretched out in front of it, and it now leapt across the carriage drive to a spot not twenty feet from where the shocked Margaret stood.

Dulwich College was — and still is — a fine public school for boys in a leafy corner of South East London. Although the College had been founded as long ago as 1619, it had moved from Dulwich Village in 1870 — only two years before our story begins — to a site on Dulwich Common. Beyond the massive wrought iron gates the splendid edifice rose majestically, fashioned in the Gothic style seen all over North Italy but not that often in South London. The façade was remarkable for the absence of stone, being made almost exclusively of brick and terracotta. Remarkable, yes, and widely remarked upon, as indeed was the College as a whole, which was admired for its graceful form and the brilliance of its design.

But when the light was fading from the sky, and the buildings of the College were swathed in shadow, it took on a melancholy appearance. Worse still, at night, and especially when the moon was high, a sensitive mind might be filled with disturbing thoughts. And on nights when the moon was full, when its sinister gleam filled the cavernous dormitories where the boarders slept, a boy might awake with a start and lie in terror, watching dark forms moving in the corners of the room, and listening to the creaking of doors and the footsteps echoing in a corridor on the floor above. At such a time, to those who were prone to fanciful imaginings, the school seemed to belong to another age. The passages joining the north and south wings to the central block of the building, which were pierced by arches, might have been cloisters in an old monastery, where cowled monks with invisible faces glided over the stone floors so softly that they might have been ghosts.

But the tall white figure lurching across the carriage drive on that dark autumn evening was real enough, and Margaret, terrified by the apparition, jumped back into the doorway. At the same time she let out a piercing scream, alarming Constance and Mary, who were coming down the stairs in order to follow her out. Even though the door was only half open, they caught a glimpse of the dreadful spectre. The spectre disappeared as suddenly as it had appeared, but in the ensuing confusion, and with only a partial view of the drive, Constance and Mary did not see in what direction it had fled. This they thought odd, because in the few seconds that had elapsed before the sinister figure bolted they had been struck by its gleaming whiteness, which made it very noticeable. In the immediate aftermath of the incident an extensive search of the garden and grounds was carried out, but it failed to unearth any sign of the ghostly intruder. It was only in the morning that further searching revealed that something or someone had been hiding in a small shrubbery near the house. The grass on the front lawn had been trodden down, and the obvious conclusion was that the figure that had so frightened young Margaret had been keeping a close eye on the door.

This was neither the first nor the last sighting of what would become known as the Peckham Ghost, which, incidentally, was always regarded as male. He had first been seen almost four weeks before the Dulwich incident in Forest Hill, outside Honor Oak Church, where he vaulted over walls and fences, pursued by a group of navvies who did not take kindly to being frightened while at work. News of the apparition spread rapidly, and the good people of South East London were rattled. Soon there were dozens of reported encounters with the ghost, who seemed to pick mainly on women and children, and from these sightings there emerged a broadly consistent picture of his physical characteristics. All his victims agreed that he was tall, although estimates ranged from six to an astonishing eight feet, depending, one presumes, on the relative height of a particular witness. He materialised from the shadows, resplendent in white and making odd noises. One little boy thought that he had sported a grey curly-haired wig, which made him a vain ghost as well as a frightening one. Peckhamites were not safe from his activities even in their own homes, for there were curious tappings and the rattling of windows and shutters in the dead of night when respectable folk were abed.

It was rumoured that the 'supernatural being' known as Spring-heeled Jack, who had given many a London servant girl a fright in the 1830s, had reappeared. This figure of urban legend was feared for his agility and swiftness and for the powerful leaps that enabled him to clear obstacles up to twenty feet high. The similarities were compelling, for the Peckham Ghost darted hither and thither, lunging and leaping like Jack. The ghost had a distinctive white uniform, just as Jack was reported to wear a black cloak over a tight-fitting white oilskin. On the other hand, Jack breathed blue fire and had glowing red eyes and clawed hands, features that were not manifested, or at least never reported, in Peckham.

Even the fit and the strong were not always safe, and the alarming experience of the Forest Hill navvies dispelled any belief that the ghost would only ever target members of the fairer sex or the younger generation. One evening, not long after the Margaret Carver encounter, a carrier trundling his wagon along Lordship Lane in East Dulwich was given a horrible fright when the ghost rushed out at him from his hiding place in a field. A report in *The Morning Advertiser* noted wryly that

the carrier was so terrified by the suddenness of the thing that instead of applying his horse-whip to good purpose — instead of leaving his mark on the miscreant in an unmistakable manner — he lashed his horses into a gallop, thus in his fright breaking the law, which says that a stage waggon shall only travel at four miles an hour.

The newspapers also speculated as to how the ghost was able to disappear so rapidly: one moment he was there, the next he was gone. Not convinced that he had supernatural origins, they suggested that he was a man dressed in a heavy overcoat, which was rather like the long garment known as an ulster. He would open the coat, flashing its white lining, and promptly close it again. Camouflaged in this way, he would slip into the gloom. And on the subject of a human identity for the ghost, it was reported by the *South London Chronicle* that

various guesses have been made as to who the fellow is. Some think that the Dulwich College boys have been mixed up in the affair, but there does not appear to be anything in support of this view. The game has by some been placed to the credit of some of the Peckham athletes, but if that is so the young men of muscle have well kept their own counsel. We have heard it whispered in a certain circle in the City, that the thing is the result of a bet, that a young fellow would play off these pranks for three months.

Several weeks of this haunting left the residents of Peckham and neighbouring areas unamused. After all, the local police — and there were certainly enough of them in Peckham — seemed no closer to catching the ghost. The officer in charge of the investigation was Inspector Arthur Gedge, a native of Suffolk and a veteran of twenty years' service. Gedge lived with his wife, Rosina, in the police house at 173 The High Street, which was next door to the police station and had in previous years been a convent and part of a mansion belonging to the wealthy Dalton family. Living with the Gedges were the *thirty-eight* policemen who made up P Division. Thirty-eight was a good number of officers, so it is not surprising that there was criticism of their failure to apprehend the spectre. Perhaps having a police house next door to a brewery tap was not the best way to concentrate the collective mind.

Nearby at 1 Bath Place in Peckham lived the family of Thomas Ayres, a labourer. One day towards the end of November little Matilda Ayres, who was twelve years old, went off with her father to catch and kill a rabbit for the family's dinner. That evening, at about eight o'clock, Matilda was sent out to dispose of the inedible bits of the rabbit. She went alone, which in view of the ghostly episodes in the neighbourhood is not what you might expect. Her errand took her past the Alliance Tavern in Sumner Road, just north of Charles Street, where a dark form loomed out from the shadows, making horrid noises and spreading its arms menacingly. Suddenly it turned white. Matilda was astonished and rushed home to tell her parents what had happened, but she could not have been all that frightened, for in as little as half an hour she was back out in the streets. Once again she saw the ghost, although this time he was lurking in John Street, which ran parallel with Charles Street. When she was asked to talk about her experience — what did the ghost look like, and what was he wearing? — she identified the garment he was wearing as a 'slop'. The word had many uses — the white clothes worn by a sailor, for example, or a butcher's apron — but in all likelihood Matilda was thinking of a countryman's white smock.

At about the same time a twelve-year-old boy by the name of Arthur Ridgway was hurrying to his home in

Bath Place, which was next door to the Ayres at no. 2. He had been dispatched to buy beer, and he had almost arrived back with a half-gallon stone bottle when the ghost leapt out at him. So thoroughly frightened was the boy that he dropped the bottle and took to his heels. But it immediately crossed his mind that, no matter how frightening a ghost in the streets of Peckham might have been, his father, who was waiting in Bath Place for some liquid refreshment after a hard day's labouring, was even more frightening. And so he sprinted back to rescue the bottle. Of course, he was now bound to meet the ghost again, but, having encountered him already, he had at least half an idea of what he was going to see. Only this time the ghost looked different, for on his head he was wearing a curly-haired wig — *the* curly-haired wig we heard about earlier.

News of these local sightings brought men and boys out on to the street. Thankfully there is no suggestion that they were carrying pitchforks and mattocks in the manner of villagers in pursuit of a local vampire, but their blood was up, and the ghost was eventually run to ground. When the angry crowd caught up with him, he was trying to gain admittance to a house in Sumner Road. Disappointingly, he did not pass through a closed door, and, as if to prove that he was human after all, he allowed himself to be arrested by two police constables. When they frisked the prisoner, the bobbies found that he had stuffed a quantity of dried peas into his pockets, the purpose of which they could not immediately divine.

On Friday the 6th of December the Peckham Ghost appeared before the magistrate, George Chance, at Lambeth Police Court. He identified himself as Joseph Munday, a labourer aged forty-three. When he was asked where he lived, he admitted that he had no fixed abode, and by now no one would have been foolish enough to understand him to mean that he slept in graveyards. He was charged first with loitering in Bath Place, and then with frightening Matilda Ayres, Arthur Ridgway and others with 'menaces and gestures'. Inspector Gedge confirmed that there had been numerous complaints about the 'ghost' in the last month. The arresting officer, Police Constable Hills, on being asked to give his account of events, said that when apprehended Munday was wearing a dark overcoat with a long white smock underneath — a smock of exactly the kind Matilda Ayres thought that he had been wearing. Hills added that Munday was also carrying a two-foot stick wrapped in another black overcoat. Munday was ordered to unbutton his coat, revealing a long white smock.

Smock or no smock, popular descriptions of the ghostly figure did not match the real Joseph Munday. He was said to be brawny and singular looking, although none of the newspaper accounts explained in any detail what made him look singular. Joseph declared that he was as innocent as a newborn baby. He flatly denied that he threw the peas found in his pockets at the windows of houses in order to frighten the occupants in the middle of the night — he carried peas on his person simply to have something to eat if he felt peckish. And he certainly would not have worn his white slop if he had foreseen that it would land him in court. He explained that he had called at Bath Place to visit a man called Hall, and, when Hall was not in, he had found himself set upon and arrested.

The court heard from a man who claimed that at one time Munday had lived next door but one to him in a street overlooking the Grand Surrey Canal, which passed nearby. Really, though, Munday was a drifter. There was little that could be done about him. Mr Chance bailed him to keep the peace at the princely sum of ten pounds, but he had no money, and he was put into custody for six months. Finally the Peckham Ghost had been laid to rest.

A Voice from Beyond

A LARGE DETACHED house situated on the north side of Wandsworth Common might have been the perfect setting for a spine-chilling tale by the master of the Victorian ghost story, M. R. James, or by his more recent counterpart, Susan Hill, who created the sinister Eel Marsh House, where poor Arthur Kipps came so badly unstuck. Of course, the streets of suburban South London are no answer to echoing monasteries or desolate causeways. But when darkness falls over the Common, or when a chilling autumn fog cloaks its empty expanses, there is reason enough to feel more than a bit on edge.

What follows is the story of the resident of this house in Wandsworth. There are no creaking floorboards nor any pale figures glimpsed in shadowy corridors. But the story is no less strange and disturbing for that. The house stood in Spanish Close, a stone's throw from the Common, and at the time, which was the year 1883, it was occupied by Charles Henry Kelly and his family. Kelly, who was originally from Salford, was forty-nine years old. His wife, whose name was Eleanor, came from Sheffield and was forty-one. With them lived their two sons, Arthur Henry and Charles Ernest, who were aged fourteen and twelve and were both at school. The family was prosperous enough to have two domestic servants, Eliza Banks and Mary Ann Lindsay, who were both in their twenties and unmarried. Eliza was a local girl, but Mary Ann, the daughter of a Chelsea pensioner who may well have seen active service in the Crimea, came from Kent.

And so it would appear that Charles Henry Kelly was every inch the middle-class Victorian. He was also a minister in the Wesleyan Methodist Church, and a photograph taken in old age shows him in a plain coat with a clerical collar. His bushy eyebrows are only a little less startling than his luxuriant sideburns, which sweep down the sides of his face like the cheekpieces of a Roman legionary's helmet. His confident smile suggests a man who has lived his live free of cares. However, that was not the case. Far from it.

To set the scene for Kelly's story, we need to take a quick look at his life and work. Although he started out as a clerk at the Board of Highways in Manchester, he soon changed direction, and by the time he was in his early twenties he had trained for the ministry. In due course he came south, and for a while he worked as an army chaplain. Then in his mid-thirties he was appointed to the Chelsea Circuit as an itinerant preacher, which kept him busy for three years. Further circuit appointments followed, first in Wandsworth and later in Westminster, each of these lasting a further three years.

As part of his work on the Wandsworth Circuit, Kelly took over management of the boys' reform school in Spanish Road, which was close to the family home. The school had a hundred and eighty residents who had been convicted in the courts, in most cases for theft or troublemaking, and given reformatory sentences of between two and five years. The solid citizens who lived in the neighbourhood may have bristled at having these ne'er-do-wells on their doorstep, but the good Wesleyan minister maintained that removing these young offenders from 'vicious associations' — a phrase he used in his memoirs — and allowing them to develop good characters was preferable to the 'penal machinery of the State'. He was proud of the fact that many of these boys enlisted, that many emigrated, and that a good number found trades.

He listened sympathetically to the boys' stories. They were unhappy creatures with troubled pasts. It was almost as if the sun was setting on their young lives, the shadows of hopelessness already falling on them, as on winter afternoons the shadows fell all too soon over the empty streets of Wandsworth, where Kelly walked lost in melancholy thought. Moved by tales of poverty, he petitioned the Home Secretary for clemency towards those who had been at the reformatory but still ended up in prison. In later life he remembered two boys who had died at the school, saddened that one had looked on him as the only real friend he had ever had, happy that the other had been reconciled with an estranged brother in the hours before his death.

These anecdotes certainly suggest that Kelly looked for the good in all people — not that he always found it in the young residents at the reform school — and that he believed in the value of helping those who deserved to be helped. One wonders if he considered that he himself was also deserving of help. Maybe yes, maybe no. But on one particular occasion he was so very fortunate, and had so lucky an escape, that he might reasonably have reckoned that he had earned at least some divine protection.

In February 1883, in his capacity as a Methodist minister, Kelly was appointed to visit the Channel Islands. He was to preach in Jersey on Sunday the 4th, and to address meetings of fellow ministers there on Monday the 5th and in Guernsey on Wednesday the 7th. His plan was to cross over from Southampton on the Friday before the first of the Jersey appointments. As the ferry was scheduled to leave at midnight, he decided to travel down from Waterloo on the night train.

But on the day of his planned departure Kelly began to feel uneasy. Instead of looking forward to a relaxing train journey from Waterloo down to the coast, with a newspaper and a book or two to keep him entertained, followed by the pleasure of sleeping in a cosy cabin on the night-time sea-crossing, he felt himself growing agitated. Although he was not really sure what was bothering him, he was in no doubt that what he was experiencing was a sense of foreboding, the fear that something unwanted and decidedly unpleasant was going to happen. No, not just the fear: the expectation, almost the certainty. And the sensation was so vivid, and so unsettling, that even when he sat down to write about this episode for his memoirs almost thirty years after the event, he could recall precisely what he had believed was happening to him. He was firmly in the grip of a presentiment of — and there was only one word for it — danger, and the danger lay ahead of him on his journey across the sea to Jersey and Guernsey. 'As if voices of the unseen' — and he must have recalled his feelings of fear as he wrote these words — 'as if voices of the unseen warned me not to go.'

The poor man was already in a state of some anxiety when a telegram arrived that afternoon. The hour of departure — the start of the fateful journey that would take him first to Waterloo, and from Waterloo to Southampton, and from Southampton to whatever lay in store — was fast approaching. He tore open the telegram, seeing to his great surprise that it had been sent from Torquay, where a sister-in-law, who was an invalid, was residing. The message was abrupt in the manner of all telegrams, and it was as blunt as it was brief: DO NOT CROSS TO JERSEY TONIGHT STOP

So it was with mixed feelings that Kelly prepared to board the Southampton train at Waterloo Station on the evening of the 2nd of February. Earlier he had decided not to set too much store by the warnings, but, as he walked to the far end of the platform and back, he felt unsettled again. He could not quite put his finger on it: the train simply did not look right. Inventing a plausible reason for cancelling his visit, he wrote two notes of apology, which the guard promised to hand to the steward of the ferry to be delivered to his hosts in Jersey and Guernsey. He then returned to Wandsworth, and we may well imagine that he wondered on the journey home if he had made the right decision after all.

The train from Waterloo pulled into Southampton Docks — without Kelly, of course — and the passengers boarded the SS *Hilda*, a mail service steamship owned by the London and South Western Railway. At midnight the *Hilda*, commanded by a Captain Merrells, headed out into the Solent, steaming down to the Yarmouth Roads off the Isle of Wight on her way westward to the Needles.

And there the *Hilda*, all eight hundred and twenty-one tons of her, ran stem on into a French fishing boat. A terrible gale had been blowing all that day, and the

fishing boat had run up through the Needles to find
shelter. Now, on impact with the steamship, she sank
immediately, with all hands going down with her.
Captain Merrells, witnessing the disaster from the
bridge of the *Hilda*, ordered a boat out in the hope of
saving the lives of the fishermen, and immediately the
second and third officers, accompanied by two seamen
and a steward, set off into the dark. They were soon lost
to view, and, when they failed to return, Merrells began
to fear that they too had succumbed to the gale. Then,
having no choice, he returned to Southampton, where he
shipped some men to replace his missing crew and set
out again for the Channel Islands.

Meanwhile a tug, the *Fawn*, had been chartered by the
marine superintendent of the London and South
Western Railway to search the scene of the collision. The
crew of the tug found some wreckage from the stricken
fishing vessel — a table that had been pitched into the
sea when the steamship crashed down on it — but
nothing by which it might be identified. However, the
men who had set out from the *Hilda* in the rescue boat
were found to be alive in spite of their ordeal, having
drifted on the wind and landed about two miles east of
Yarmouth. They gratefully boarded the *Fawn*, and, when

the *Hilda* passed down the Roads on her second journey out, they changed places with the emergency crew, who returned with the tug to Southampton.

That afternoon Kelly learnt about the tragedy when he heard the cry of a newspaper boy selling evening papers. 'Dreadful collision in the Channel!' the boy was shouting. 'Loss of life!' As these sombre words came floating through the gathering gloom, Kelly realised that he had indeed been spared a terrible experience. But if he thought that he had been right to stay at home, others were not so sure, and one day he received a letter from an acquaintance in Guernsey questioning his decision not to travel on that fateful night. What would be thought of a general, his correspondent asked, who ordered his troops to turn back on the eve of battle? Kelly replied that only a fool would think that the general should have risked his life and the lives of his men. 'A wise man,' he continued, 'would remember that a battle is not a campaign, and he might avoid one that he might live to fight many more.'

Still, the question remains why Kelly had been swayed by his sense of foreboding. A possible answer is that he experienced what is referred to as precognition, or future vision. Science dismisses the phenomenon on the grounds that realising that something will happen before it has happened is putting the effect before the cause. However, there are many attested cases. One of the grisliest involved the brutal kidnapping and murder of the baby son of the aviator Charles Lindbergh in 1932. Well over a thousand members of the public claimed to have 'seen' the tragedy in advance in dreams. Could it be that Kelly's dithering as he walked along the platform at Waterloo was another instance of precognition?

Then again, was his sense of looming disaster a case not of precognition but of déjà vu? After all, there had been atrocious weather in the shipping lanes in January, and the newspapers were full of grim accounts of incidents in the English Channel. One vessel capsized off Plymouth. Another, carrying a cargo of sugar and rum, was wrecked on the Kent coast. Yet another went down off the Scilly Isles with the loss of thirty-five lives. It is possible that Kelly had read about recent tragedies, and was haunted by images of splintering timbers and drowning men as he contemplated his own journey in the days ahead.

However, he may have had more personal and more distressing reasons for listening to his inner voice. For he and his wife had suffered a terrible loss when their first child, a daughter by the name of Blanche, died at the age of five. Had the desperate need to remain in some sort of contact with the little girl predisposed Kelly to believe in a world of spirits? Quite possibly. But a further incident — the John Stirling incident — must surely have pushed him in that direction.

Kelly had been acquainted with John Stirling at school, although he, Kelly, was older by two years. One Sunday in 1854, the 5th of November to be exact, he had been preaching at Rixton, a village that is now in Cheshire but was then in Lancashire. Walking home afterwards with a friend, John Hardey, Kelly described a strange dream in which he had seen a boy lying dead on the ground. Kelly recognised the boy as John Stirling, who would have been eighteen. And at that moment he was certain that the poor fellow was dead.

A while later he happened to read an announcement in *The Manchester Guardian* that made his blood run cold. As one might expect, all the talk in the newspapers in that year was of the Crimean War, and reports of the Battle of Inkerman were beginning to appear in their pages. This fierce engagement had taken place on the 5th of November, that is to say the very same day on which Kelly had described his dream to Hardey. And now in the *Guardian* he read for the first time that Lieutenant John Stirling of the 41st Foot — 'holding the colours of his regiment' — had fallen on the fog-bound field of battle.

Kelly had been devoted to Stirling, and in his memoirs there is a poignant reference to a letter sent from Scotland by his young friend that he had kept for many years, though the paper had long since yellowed. But even when weighed down with life's sadnesses, he derived great comfort from what he called 'unseen presences'. He was convinced that communion with the departed was a preparation for his own death, an assurance that heaven would be 'a place of familiar sights, familiar music, familiar faces'. And although he did not think of himself as being in any sense psychic, he was still enough of a believer in the supernatural to pay serious attention to those experiences — what we might call premonitions, or anticipations, or warnings — that were in any ordinary way inexplicable.

The irony, of course, is that Kelly would have survived the disaster along with all the passengers and crew of the *Hilda*, which had returned to Southampton without loss of life. In a way his premonitions were wasted on him. How much better if the poor wretches on the French fishing boat had been warned off the sea.

If they had been as prescient as Charles Henry Kelly, they might have been on the lookout for steamships looming out of the darkness on a winter's night. And how much better if young John Stirling had been gifted with his former schoolfellow's foresight, for then he might have kept clear of the bullet or the cannonball that laid him low on the rain-swept field of Inkerman.

Haunted Houses in Stamford Street

AT ABOUT HALF-PAST two in the afternoon of a rainy
Monday in January 1863 a crowd gathered outside a
huddle of houses in Stamford Street in South London.
Not for the first time, either, for a crowd standing
outside these particular residences was not an unusual
sight. As a rule, though, this happened later in the day
when it was dark. And when it was dark in that very
nasty part of the capital, on the notoriously dangerous
south side of the river, anyone out and about needed
nerves of steel. The streets were unlit. The doorways
were shadowy and menacing. The passages between
houses reached so far into the dark that, for all anyone
knew, they might have led down into subterranean
places deep beneath the earth. And if night-time south

of the river in the nineteenth century was not already bad enough, it was all the worse for the goings-on in Stamford Street.

Stamford Street linked Blackfriars Road in Southwark to Waterloo Road in Lambeth, following the line of the river. You would certainly not go there for the scenery: Stamford Street, as one writer noted, was inhospitable and thoroughly gloomy in aspect. Many of the dwellings were lodging houses, and on any day of the week, before the sun rose fully, or after dark, you might see a cart laden with a few possessions ready to do a moonlight flit, or, in the language of the Victorian streets, to 'moonshine it'.

The house at the heart of this story, which was at no. 43, was more run-down than most of the others in Stamford Street, and there was a reason for this, and consequences too. The exterior of the house was utterly forlorn. The doors and window frames were dirty and riddled with rot, and not a single pane of glass remained intact. The basement area was completely choked with rubbish, and it was widely acknowledged in the neighbourhood that the inside of the house was no less neglected than the outside. The furniture, which would once have been considered elegant, was crumbling into dust, and rats ran hither and thither without fear of human opposition.

None of this went unnoticed, and there were many complaints about the house, and indeed about two others that stood at the same end of Stamford Street, which was the Blackfriars Road end. They were in a similar state of dilapidation, and no one was happy about it. A man who called himself 'The Grumbler' complained in the *South London Times* about the state of things in his part of the metropolis. He complained, for example, that not all the streets were properly paved. He also complained that people were relieving themselves in the street. *And* he complained about the three ruined houses at the corner of Stamford Street and Blackfriars Road, which he considered a disgrace. Not only were they a danger to passers-by — a strong gust of wind would surely send the roofs tumbling into the road below — but they were an eyesore. 'A dust heap would be quite as picturesque,' he thundered, 'and a great deal more useful in such a neighbourhood.'

Dilapidated buildings were not unknown in the capital, so why the crowds? The 1863 incident with which we started will come up again later, but the important point to make here is that rumours about the three houses were rife, and the rumour that got a firmer grip on the popular imagination than any other was that they were haunted. And the house that is the real subject of our story was not simply believed to be haunted but *known* to be haunted, and the reason, as anyone in the crowds that regularly assembled would have told you, was as follows. When darkness fell, the ghostly shape of a woman could be seen inside the house. In fact there were occasions when what was seen was the ghostly shapes of *two* women. She or they could be seen clearly through the windows, for the curtains, if there had ever been any, had completely rotted away. And the shape, or the shapes, could be seen flitting through the rooms, dressed from head to toe in white and lit by a flickering light.

Nor were these the only disturbing manifestations. A muffin man who happened to be passing along the street claimed that he heard ghostly bells being rung in the empty rooms of the crumbling house. And a charwoman swore that a ghost rushed out one Saturday night and gave her a terrible scare. She — the charwoman, that is, not the ghost — had been on her way home, carrying a jug of ale under her apron. She was so alarmed that she fell to the pavement, spraining her ankle.

As if to add to the general mystery surrounding the house in Stamford Street, only the neighbours knew that it was inhabited. One of the occupants — it was reported that there were two — was Miss Cordelia Angelica Read. She was heartily disliked, which had a lot to do with the neglected state of her property. But she was also a recluse: she never received visitors into her home and only rarely ventured forth. And when she did venture forth, she was seen to be as dusty and decayed as the house — the haunted house — in which she eked out what the world thought must have been a lonely and squalid existence. Tales were told about the emaciated Miss Read, that she lived in filth and ate nothing but stale buns, which, it was popularly supposed, she got from John Pring's bakery at no. 47. No, the neighbours really had very little time for Cordelia, and, when she died in old age on Wednesday the 6th of December 1871, few if any tears would have been shed in Stamford Street, or in Blackfriars Road, or, for that matter, anywhere in Southwark or Lambeth.

The true story of the haunted house centres around a creative family, their quarrels and their law cases, and a very considerable endowment that made possible the building of the south block of the Brompton Hospital for

Consumption and Diseases of the Chest. Cordelia came from a rather remarkable family, which may come as a surprise given all that has been said about her. Her grandparents on her mother's side were Isabella and Edward Beetham, the former a famous silhouettist, and the latter a resourceful jack of all trades who was at various times an actor, a designer of safety curtains for theatres, a publisher, an insurance agent, and the inventor of the Beetham's Patent Washing Mill.

Their eldest daughter, Jane, who was Cordelia's mother, inherited Isabella's artistic talents and worked alongside her. She was a miniaturist and studied under a family friend, the Cornish artist John Opie, who in due course asked her father for his permission to marry her. Edward Beetham declined to give it. Possibly he felt that Opie's discreditable history — he had divorced his first wife — would combine with his own murky past — he and Isabella had eloped — to involve the family in unnecessary scandal. But in the end Jane managed to marry respectably, in 1800, either through personal choice or on account of parental pressure. Her husband was John Read, a wealthy widowed solicitor. Jane was in her twenties and John in his thirties, and their only child, a daughter, was born early in 1801. The family lived north of the river for many years, but in 1827 they moved down to Stamford Street, where John owned a great deal of property.

While the Reads resided at no. 22, the other houses were left unoccupied, which may explain why John, who could have made good money renting them out, was considered to be eccentric in some quarters. On his death in 1847 he left his personal estate to Jane and his real estate, which was substantial, to Cordelia. Mother and daughter moved to no. 43, where they lived together for another ten years with one or two resident servants. Although the houses were in a poor state of repair, Mrs and Miss Read were not entirely negligent. They made a point of inspecting the properties on a nightly basis in order to ensure that everything was locked and nothing was missing, and it was this nocturnal habit that gave rise to the story of the haunted house. The two 'ghosts', who drew so many crowds and generated so much tittle-tattle, were none other than Jane and Cordelia gliding from room to room, candles in hand and possibly dressed in white.

Over the course of the years their Stamford Street estate suffered at least one burglary. In 1846 a young fellow by the name of James Fling attempted, unsuccessfully, to steal a copper boiler and a quantity of lead from one of the houses, receiving a twelve-month prison sentence for his pains. But this curiously lax state of affairs continued into the next generation, and in 1863 a Mary Cornish of 41 Hatfield Street, which intersected Stamford Street, declared that she and not Cordelia was the rightful owner of the estate. Supported by a mob she broke into several houses, and laid claim to them by saying 'Now show us your title deeds'. There seemed to be considerable ill-feeling towards Cordelia: on one occasion the elderly lady was forced to escape from the mob over the rooftops. In court she explained that the houses had been neglected since the time of her father. She had thought about carrying out repairs, but collecting the rent from her other properties, which were scattered all over London, meant that she did not have the time to see to them. Meanwhile Mary and some of her supporters were found guilty of unlawfully occupying nos. 1, 2, 3, 5, 19, 20 and 22 Stamford Street, which all belonged to Cordelia Read.

At the end of 1871 Cordelia fell ill. She was seventy, and her servant, Susan Goring, who had been with her for two or three years, called for Henry Johnson, a doctor with a practice in York Road. Concerned that the elderly lady was living in such an abandoned state, Dr Johnson asked her about her relatives. She took umbrage at his interference, dismissed him, and summoned instead Dr Edwin Canton, the house surgeon at Charing Cross Hospital. Within days she was found dead in her chair in the back room. She was buried on the 14th of December 1871 at Kensal Green Cemetery alongside her parents.

Following her death it was revealed that Cordelia was not as poor as her living conditions might suggest. For one thing, she was able to employ servants. Then again, although her house was filthy, it was full of fine furniture, which local gossip had been wrong to describe as decrepit. There was Georgian silverware on the sideboards, and there were paintings on the walls. Susan Goring asserted that her mistress had been so far from subsisting on stale buns as to have enjoyed a diet of brown bread and pastries, meat and vegetables, and port.

Cordelia's individuality could not be denied — the dirt and decay, the room full of hats and bonnets from a bygone age, the canvas bag with five hundred pounds in sixpenny, fourpenny and threepenny pieces — but she had been as sharp as a knife. She was curmudgeonly but also determined, and on her death she still owned at least eight of her father's Stamford Street properties, and had thousands of pounds in the bank and in stocks and shares. Her personal possessions included furniture, paintings, trinkets and jewellery. In fact she was a very wealthy woman with assets of one hundred and twenty thousand pounds, which today would be worth *thirteen million* pounds.

She never married and had no direct descendants, so her wider family expected to inherit. But Cordelia had other ideas. In her will she left the greater part of her personal wealth to the Brompton Hospital for Consumption and Diseases of the Chest. The family stepped in to challenge the will, demanding to be told if the deceased had been *compos mentis* at the time the document was drawn up. They even pushed to have the dead woman's head opened, until Dr Canton, who presumably thought that she had been perfectly on the ball, pointed out that she had been able to speak Latin, an accomplishment that must have carried a great deal of weight in Victorian times!

A family member who felt especially aggrieved was a man by the name of James Chabot, who was Cordelia's cousin once removed. His own story makes grim reading. Only weeks after his marriage, which took place in 1847, he committed adultery. He also hit his wife, knelt on her stomach, gave her two black eyes, and refused to cohabit. When his wife gave birth the following year — the child was still-born, possibly as a result of the physical violence she had endured — he was living with another woman. Then in 1859 he divorced his wife in order to marry the woman he was living with, and, although by this time Cordelia had written her will, it is more than likely that his record of unacceptable behaviour influenced her decision to leave him nothing.

James demanded an inquest. But if he was hoping to establish that Cordelia had not been in full possession of all her faculties, which would have raised questions about her will, the evidence was not forthcoming. Quite the contrary: Cordelia had let her properties disintegrate precisely in order to spite her family, with whom she had consistently fallen out. Nor was there any reason to suggest foul play, for nobody stood to benefit from her death, not even poor Susan Goring, who was left not a bean in the will. At the inquest Dr Canton explained that the old lady had died of the combined effects of bronchitis and fatty degeneration of the heart, a natural cause of death for someone of her age, and the coroner issued a statement that there were no grounds to suggest that her death was suspicious in any way.

The surviving executor, Charles Shepheard, took the family to court to ensure that Cordelia's final wishes were carried out, and in May 1872 the Right Honourable James Plaisted, Baron Penzance, pronounced the validity of the will, and the Brompton Hospital received the major share of her wealth. In time the Stamford Street tenements were sold and redeveloped. But the 'haunted' house at no. 43 had not gone away — not yet at least — and the inventory of its peculiar secrets afforded the newspapers much material. A writer in *The Morning Advertiser* was struck by the great age of everything in the house. Plates and dishes, finger-bowls and decanters, little wax dolls in a fully furnished doll's house, ebony chairs inlaid with brass, a mandolin and a lute and a harpsichord with only a ghostly reminder of the sound it had once made, embroidered silks and brocaded satins and rolls of rich damask, silk stockings and kid gloves, a rosewood card table with a pack of cards and a heap of pearl-fish counters, silver salt cellars and chased punch ladles, a pair of pretty gold bracelets and a heavy gold French watch — the list went on and on. And although these survivals of the past were quaint and romantic, they were also sad in a dusty and rather faded way. Time, it would seem, had not entirely stood still.

Madam, Don't Be Alarmed!

THE MEDICAL MAN leaned closer to Juliet Hart-Davis. 'Madam,' he began in a confiding manner, 'don't be alarmed if during the interview I should go into a trance.' His voice dropped to a murmur — a gentle and reassuring murmur. 'I am subject to that kind of thing,' he went on, 'and I shall no doubt convey to you certain messages from the spirits which will certainly interest you.'

As Juliet had already admitted to the medical man in confidence that as a child she had seen angels, she was excited by this development. All the same, she was somewhat taken aback when he clasped both her hands in his, which she would probably have regarded as an unacceptable liberty if he had not been a doctor of sorts.

Then, as she watched, his eyes closed, a great shiver ran through his body, and he fell into what she could only describe as a daze. What happened next was little short of thrilling. The doctor's 'spirit guide', a young native American girl called Winona, indicated to him by means of mysterious signs that she, Winona, was in contact with 'one who had gone before', that is to say a person who had died. That person just happened to be Juliet's late mother, Anne Heurtley, who had shuffled off her mortal coil three years previously. Although the conversation with Anne was a mite strange, it was clear to Juliet that it really was Mama who was speaking, for no one else would have been privy to the details of their family life, and no one else would have had access to her shameful secrets.

The year was 1879, and Juliet Hart-Davies, aged thirty-seven, was not a happy woman. Having been married at twenty-one to a man chosen for her by her mother, she spent several years in Argentina, where her husband was Inspector of Mines. In 1875 she suffered the social stigma of being divorced for adultery, the story being that she had enjoyed rather too much the company of an Italian gentleman, Roberto Armenio, on a ship steaming from Buenos Aires to Rio de Janeiro. The upshot of this faux pas was that she was no longer able to see her fourteen-year-old son, who remained in the care of her unforgiving ex-husband.

But Juliet had reason to be optimistic when two years after the divorce she met and married James Penrose Hart-Davis, a ship's-captain in the merchant navy. In financial terms, since Juliet was a rich woman, this was not regarded as an equal match. Even so, James was the son of a clergyman who had reached the heights of the archbishopric of Melbourne, and in marrying Juliet he had afforded her at least a veneer of respectability, which, given her past, was more than welcome. With the money she had at her disposal they were able to move into Farquhar Lodge, a large house of about fourteen rooms situated on a road in Upper Norwood that ran between Dulwich and Crystal Palace. Sadly, though, Juliet's new life was no more satisfactory than the old, for James, who was only thirty-nine, was unable to consummate the marriage. Contemporary records described his condition somewhat coyly as 'a chronic weakness and condition of his parts of generation'. By way of clarification it was further noted that he suffered from 'a disease of the character'. But the actual cause of his weakened private parts and ulcerated character — a venereal disease, alcoholism, a nervous disorder — was not divulged.

In the hope of recovery James consulted not only mainstream doctors but also those on the fringes of the medical profession. One of those he turned to in his search for a cure was an American gentleman by the name of John William Fletcher, who was said to use invisible natural forces to heal physical conditions, and who was variously described as a galvanist, a 'magnetic' doctor — a doctor specialising in magnotherapy — and a mesmerist. During the treatment sessions James let Fletcher into his confidence, either because he positively wanted to, or because in his trance-state his judgement deserted him. As well as talking freely about his unsatisfactory marriage to Juliet, he gave an account of Juliet's background, not omitting to mention the fact that she had been brought up in a splendid mansion called Hampton Court House, and that she was a very rich woman who had inherited in the region of a hundred thousand pounds. Some of the inheritance, he added for good measure, came from Juliet's mother, and the rest from a family friend.

James persuaded Juliet that she too could benefit from seeing Fletcher, who would be able to help her with her nervous headaches. Juliet readily agreed, having been brought up with knowledge of and access to alternative therapies through her father, Richard Walter Heurtley, who, after starting as a clerk at the Bank of England, became the honorary secretary of the Homeopathic Society and later trained as a homeopath in America. She found John William Fletcher both charming and persuasive. Quite apart from being a handsome man with a full head of dark hair and magnificent Dundreary whiskers, he was a believer in and practitioner of spiritualism, and after their initial consultation he visited Juliet at her home at least twice a week for three guineas a pop. He — and Winona — granted Juliet an entrée into the spirit world, and it was rumoured that he gave her a lot of attention as well, much of it of an intimate nature.

Juliet's mother Anne proved to be an accommodating spirit. She was frequently present — not in the flesh, of course — and very chatty. She was also pleased to be reunited with her daughter. 'Your séance of yesterday made me very happy,' she was once heard to say. 'It brought back former memories, and these were very acceptable.' She assured Juliet that there were better times ahead. 'Some troubles will yet visit you,' she said, 'but your future will become happier in time.' Juliet was astonished that her mother's spirit shared so many of the same opinions as Mr Fletcher. Both obviously had her best interests at heart, and, when Mr Fletcher began suggesting that her relationship with James Hart-Davies was not doing her any good, her mother was quick to agree. 'Your present life is unsuitable and is wearing you away,' Anne's spirit said to her, 'because your nerve power is continually being thrown off without any return of the necessary vital powers.' Although Juliet recorded in writing the outcome of the séances and the conversations with her mother, she did not comment on whether the old woman had always been quite so verbose. Maybe the late Mrs Heurtley's prolixity had come upon her on the other side, as it were.

At this point Mr Fletcher introduced his wife to Juliet, who by then was delighted with the way the séances were progressing. A short and rather stout lady, Susan Willis Fletcher was widely known as a spiritualist both in England, where she now lived, and in America, where she had been born, and where the whole phenomenon of spiritualism had also been born. The key date in the history of the movement was the year 1848, when the Fox family of Hydesville, New York, moved into a new house that was reputed to be haunted. Two of the six Fox children, Kate and Maggie, who were aged fourteen and eleven, began using a system of raps to communicate with a spirit who went by the name of Charles B. Rosna. Using the Fox sisters as his mouthpiece, Rosna explained that he was an itinerant pedlar, and that five years previously he had been brutally murdered and buried in the cellar of the family's home. From these remarkable beginnings spiritualism grew to provide its many adherents with two comforting beliefs, the first of which was that there was life after death, and the second that the dead could be communicated with. In 1888 — some years after our story — Maggie Fox admitted that it was all a hoax. A year later, under pressure from the spiritualism fraternity, she retracted her confession. As for Charles B. Rosna, he has remained beyond the reach of researchers. A few bones were found in the celebrated cellar, but it is not possible to determine whether their owner was of the spiritualist persuasion, or of some other persuasion, or of no persuasion at all. Bones are bones.

The Fletchers, who were spirited as well as spiritualist, quickly became firm friends with Juliet, and they were invited to stay the night at Farquhar Lodge and to dine with her at the nearby Crystal Palace. What James thought about this intimate friendship is not entirely clear, but Juliet was fortunate enough to win the approval of Spirit-Mama. 'Cultivate your natural longings for spiritual intercourse,' was Anne Heurtley's advice, delivered from a very great distance, 'and the "cheerful society" of spiritualists.' Before long Juliet was calling Fletcher 'Brother Willie' and his wife 'Sister Susie'. Her mother approved of these monikers too. 'Oh yes, for I love them the same,' she assured Juliet, 'as if they were actually family.'

As a sign of the high regard in which she held Susan, Juliet showed her the beautiful and expensive jewellery she had inherited from her mother, an item of which was a fine necklace set with diamonds and amethysts. Following this display of intimacy Juliet received a grave warning from Spirit-Mama that she must never wear those jewels again, for they were imbued with her mother's strong magnetism, a power that would harm her. The shade of Anne Heurtley went on to propose that it would be better by far for Juliet to entrust the jewels to Susan's safekeeping. But on this occasion Juliet decided to ignore her mother's warning. She was particularly fond of that necklace.

Again, what James Hart-Davies thought of it all is not known. But he may have cursed his late mother-in-law when she gave Juliet her blessing from beyond the grave to leave him, take all her valuable property, and move to 22 Gordon Street in Bloomsbury, which was the home of the Fletchers. Juliet, who was a considerate guest, offered the Fletchers her annual allowance of three hundred pounds to help with household expenses. It was said that the Fletchers for their part made it apparent that the new freedom Juliet was to enjoy with them embraced the doctrine of free love, which could be conducted in the privacy of their Bloomsbury home without the tut-tuttings they had to put up with in other corners of London society. Many spiritualists not only approved of but also practised free love, which was defined rather evasively by John Russell Bartlett in his 1859 *Dictionary of Americanisms* as the 'freedom of the affections' and the 'right to consort with those with whom we have "elective affinities", regardless of the shackles of matrimony'. As if to illustrate the potency of the doctrine in the Fletcher household, a second lodger, by the name of Morton, who was officially the Fletchers' legal advisor, was also said to be Susan's lover. These complex arrangements looked set to become even more entangled when it was suggested that Juliet and Fletcher had indulged in improper relations. Juliet would later deny that anything of the sort had happened. She also denied that a certain Captain Lindmark was her lover, *and* that she had enjoyed a romance on board a steam ship with an Italian gentleman.

Juliet was frequently invited by Fletcher to a Gordon Street séance to communicate with the dear departed. The séance room was furnished simply with a couch, window blinds, gas lights, and a small table upholstered in red velvet. On one occasion, having turned the lights down low, Fletcher got ready for Winona or his other spirit guide, Doctor, to make an appearance. In the gloom a rapid rapping on the walls was heard. When Juliet asked what was happening, Fletcher calmly explained that the spirit wished to communicate with her in writing this time, and as he said this the small side table on the far side of the room began to move slowly towards them, one jerky leg at a time. Susan then entered the room. Her hand would do the writing under the control of Dewdrop, who was her own spirit guide. Dewdrop was a native American girl, like Winona. Should we be surprised that the two 'girls' were insanely jealous of each other?

Falling into a trance, Susan began to write a message that Dewdrop was passing on from Juliet's mother. 'Dear Juliet,' the message read, 'do as you are instructed by me.' Juliet took the peevish tone of the message to mean that her mother was annoyed that her previous instructions about the disposal of the diamonds and amethysts had been ignored. With a sigh, and without hesitation, she handed her precious jewels to Susan. Not that the matter ended there, for in time most of Juliet's belongings were moved from Upper Norwood to Bloomsbury. Jewellery, expensive dresses, lace, furs inherited from Anne — all these passed into the care of the Fletchers. When Susan began to wear the beautiful items without a by-your-leave, a message was received that Anne did not mind. She was more concerned that her daughter put her affairs in order to prepare for the afterlife, which would be most effectively done by making a will in favour of, yes, Susan Willis Fletcher. As luck would have it, just when a lawyer was needed, Morton was on hand to draft something suitably legal.

Even as her spiritual life flourished, Juliet's health declined. She suffered fainting fits, which often came on after drinking from a little teapot the Fletchers set aside for her exclusive use, and, when they also began to starve her, she grew progressively thinner. However, it was this very weakness that probably saved Juliet's life. The Fletchers were due to return to America to attend a conference at the spiritualist campground at Lake Pleasant in the town of Montague in Massachusetts. They could not risk leaving Juliet behind — she would be beyond their influence, and might even be persuaded to return to James Hart-Davies and rewrite her will — so they took her with them. While she was in America, Juliet met another spiritual advisor, the self-styled Dr James McGeary, who persuaded her that the Fletchers were fraudsters. McGeary saw to it that Juliet got some of her belongings back. He then helped her to return to England.

Back in London a law case was brought against the Fletchers: six charges of obtaining goods by false pretences and one of obtaining goods by witchcraft and sorcery. Whereas John William Fletcher had the sense to remain in America, his wife Susan Willis Fletcher came to London to answer the charges. She believed that it was her duty to defend the cause of spiritualism against the doubters and the haters. After a long hearing — but only a short period of deliberation — the Old Bailey jury found her guilty of most of the charges. She received a one-year custodial sentence, having served which she returned to America, where she published a defence of herself, at great length, in a book with the inspired title *Twelve Months in an English Prison*.

But the trial did nothing for Juliet's reputation, for she had been exposed as a foolish and credulous woman. Much of the rest of her life was spent in Paris, where she died in 1912. She was buried back in England in the cemetery in Walton-on-Thames not far from her childhood home.

The Screaming Spectre of Farringdon

THIS IS THE tale of a ghost whose haunt has moved over time. Indeed, she is said to have haunted two different sites at the same time. Well, we may have two different ghosts, one for each of the two sites. And possibly three, the third being a ghost who has never yet haunted, but which may well haunt on some distant day. Time, as they say, will tell.

In 1758 a widow by the name of Sarah Metyard, who was forty years old, kept a haberdasher's shop in Bruton Street in Mayfair. Now, Bruton Street was fashionable, and Sarah needed the assistance of her daughter, Sarah Morgan Metyard, who was twenty and was known as Sally. Working alongside Sally was a gaggle of young apprentices, five girls who had previously been in the care of various parish workhouses. In all likelihood they were orphans, or the children of pauper parents, who had been farmed out by the parish officers to learn a useful trade. If they had a trade, the thinking went, they would not be a burden on local ratepayers in later life. Furthermore, the cost of their board and lodging was being met by Mrs Metyard, who in turn profited by their free and unregulated labour. It seemed like a very good arrangement.

The oldest of the five apprentices were Ann Naylor and Sarah Hinchman, who were both thirteen years of age. Philadelphia Dowley was ten, and Mary Naylor, Ann's younger sister, was eight. Ann Paul's age has not survived. Since Mrs Metyard was a milliner, they might in time have been trained to make hats, although for now they were required only to make silk net purses and knit mittens. But something the girls *did* learn quickly was that Mrs Metyard was a singularly bad-tempered woman who was not particularly fond of anyone. She even abused her daughter Sally, physically as well as verbally. But her dislike was chiefly aimed at Ann Naylor, a rather sickly girl whose work was hampered by a painful whitlow on one of her hands, which it would be costly to treat.

Mrs Metyard was also mean. Those of her friends who were invited to dinner might swear in her defence that she kept a very good table, but such largesse did not extend to the wretched apprentices, who, underfed and threatened with violence, worked long hours in a small room with hardly any light or ventilation. The little girls had so little freedom that they only left the house every other Sunday, and even then under the close supervision of the Metyards, who were concerned that they might escape and report the cruel conditions they endured to the parish authorities. Ann Naylor, who was most out of favour, received the least food. The local milk boy noticed that she was ravenous and out of pity gave her free milk. Although she was desperate, she was also brave and once ran away. But she was soon caught and taken back to be bullied all over again.

Ann was not deterred, though, and one day, finding that the front door was unlocked, she made a dash for it. She was apprehended by Jeremiah Brown, the milkman. 'Pray, milkman, let me go,' she begged, 'for I have had no victuals for a long time, and if I stay here I shall be starved to death.' Brown, who delivered a generous measure of milk to Mrs Metyard every day, and knew that she spent lavishly in the local food shops, was sure the girl was exaggerating. He detained her long enough to be dragged away by Sally Metyard. Later he claimed that he had reported Sally's rough handling of the girl to a parish guardian. The parish did nothing.

Determined to break Ann's spirit once and for all, Sarah and Sally beat her furiously with a walking stick and a broom. Sally continued the punishment long after her mother ran out of puff. She seemed particularly offended by the girl's insurrection, and it may be that she was angry because she too longed to escape. Far from pitying her victim, she decided more punishment was needed and called to her mother for assistance. 'No,' Sarah replied, 'if you will have your crotchets, you must do them yourself.' Annoyed by her mother's refusal to help, Sally redoubled her efforts. She tied Ann's hands behind her back and then roped her to the door, so that she was unable to sit or lie down.

The other little apprentices were made to work in full view of Ann's discomfort as a warning. For four days the poor girl was forced to stand, with nothing to eat or drink, and only untied at night for a few hours. Her injuries and hunger prevented her from uttering any sound other than a quiet moan. After three days even the moaning stopped. Ann was bent double over the rope, but Sally, convinced that she was feigning distress, beat her again with a shoe. Ann did not so much as flinch. Calling for hartshorn smelling salts, Sarah ordered the other girls to work downstairs, while she and Sally struggled to untie the slumped body from the door. Ann Naylor was dead.

Sally suggested that they summon the parish authorities to take the body away for burial. But Sarah pointed out that anyone who saw the emaciated and mutilated corpse would realise how badly Ann had been treated. Only if it was believed that she had run away would they avoid serious trouble. And so, when the household sat down later to eat, Sarah told one of the girls to fetch Ann from the garret. Her plan worked, for the girl she had sent upstairs found the garret door open and the room empty and raised the alarm. When it was discovered that the outside door was also wide open, Sarah announced that Ann must have run away. Only she and her daughter knew that Ann was lying dead in a box they had hidden in an out of the way part of the house.

But the parish orphans were clever little things — they had to be — and they knew that Ann would have been too weak to run away. Sarah Hinchman's suspicions were confirmed when she was given all three of the missing girl's shifts, which clearly showed her laundry mark. Without these she would not have got far. Then Philly Dowley discovered that Ann's only pair of shoes was still in the house. No one would leave such a precious commodity behind, especially with winter coming. Even little Mary Naylor whispered to one of the lodgers that she was certain that her sister was dead. When the lady of the house got to hear this, she turned on Philly, who was the source of the rumour. 'Miss Death,' she hissed menacingly, 'I shall call you Miss Death.' However, when a second girl was silenced a year later, it was not Philly but little Mary Naylor. She had been badly beaten and starved before being killed, and, although it is understandable that the other apprentices lived in fear, the sad fact is that her death was not reported. No one seemed to care that she and her sister had disappeared.

Six weeks after Ann's disappearance the stench of decomposition was becoming so obvious that Sarah decided to chop up the body and burn it in the fireplace. Opening the box, she set to work on the disfigured hand, her thinking being that the whitlow might reveal the victim's identity. This business, though, was so foul smelling and time consuming that she was forced to devise a new plan, namely to throw the dead girl's remains into the great Fleet Sewer, which would carry them down into the Thames. As it happened, she knew the very place where she could access the sewer — Chick Lane in Farringdon — for she was blessed with local knowledge. She had been living there when, as Sarah Cook, she married Morgan Metyard, a painter, in the nearby church of St Andrew's. Farringdon in those days was a notorious slum. Lying west of Smithfield, east of Fagin's Field Lane haunt, and north of Newgate prison, it had an unenviable reputation for its thieves' hideouts and its houses of ill-fame. Levels of crime were high, and people were reluctant to report suspicious goings-on to the authorities.

But over the years the area had changed. High walls had been built to contain the sewer, which made it impossible for Sarah to dispose of her grisly cargo in the way she intended. But while she was fretting over what to do with the body, she noticed a filthy gulley leading through a grating down to the sewer, which to her lazy way of thinking was the obvious place to dump poor Ann's remains. Even if the body parts were discovered, nothing would link them to a respectable Mayfair milliner, especially when Farringdon overflowed with criminals, any one of whom was capable of so vile a crime.

Sarah headed to the Haunch of Venison tavern near Temple Bar for a restorative brandy, but she left in a huff when the landlord complained that she had brought an awful smell into his establishment. Her clothes had of course been befouled by the putrefying mess she had scraped into the gulley, which, incidentally, some horrified night watchmen stumbled upon that very evening. The parish overseer was called to collect the remains, but there was no inquest, for the local coroner thought that the child must have been the victim not of a murderer but of an anatomist keen to practise his skills. The order was given to bury the remains, and that would have been that but for the fact that relations between Sarah and Sally Metyard continued to deteriorate.

One man who noticed how poorly mother and daughter got on was Richard Rooker, a sixty-year-old grocer formerly of Water Lane, off Fleet Street. When he decided to retire to a more exclusive address, his choice of lodgings just happened to be the home of the Metyards. This was in 1759. But when he saw how Sarah Metyard treated her apprentices — a state of affairs he disliked but did not exactly oppose — he soon moved out. Since he also felt sorry for Sally, he took her with him, ostensibly as his servant but more likely as his mistress. First they set up home not far off in Hill Street, but the mother's habit of turning up on a daily basis to harangue the elderly grocer drove him to retreat to a property he owned in Ealing. Distance obviously did not deter Sarah, and on one of her unwelcome visits to Ealing she threw caution to the wind, calling Rooker a perfumed tea merchant, which was quite an insult. In response Sally said that Sarah was the Chick Lane Ghost and would do well to remember the gulley-hole, an unfortunate comment that made Rooker prick up his ears. Sally later explained to him what had happened, naturally failing to mention her part in the murder. Rooker was a fool for Sally's charms and he trusted her version of events. He felt that the mother had to be punished — a way of getting her out of his hair — and so he wrote a letter to the authorities at Tottenham High Cross, the Naylor sisters' parish.

However, Rooker had misjudged the matter, and in 1762 an investigation into the heinous crime led to *both* the Metyards being arrested. Throughout the trial Sarah insisted that Ann Naylor had simply run away, while

Sally declared that she had acted under the influence of an evil, abusive mother. Their lies availed them not, and they were sentenced to be hanged at Tyburn on the 28th of July and then publicly dissected at Surgeons' Hall.

Before they could be executed, the priest at Newgate thought it his Christian duty to reconcile mother and daughter. But they were more concerned to escape the noose. Sally falsely and unsuccessfully claimed that she was pregnant. Sarah, somewhat ironically, decided to starve herself to death to cheat the executioner, as a result of which, on the evening of the 27th, she suffered a fit and lapsed into unconsciousness. The following day she would not have been aware that she had been loaded into a cart with her daughter to be taken to Tyburn through hostile and hissing crowds, and in fact she was still comatose when she was strung up on the gallows. All the while Sally looked out for her lover, hoping that he might somehow obtain a pardon for her, but, when she met her end, Rooker was nowhere to be seen.

And what of the ghosts? Perhaps it is no wonder that there are no tales of remorseful Metyards haunting Tyburn, or the site of the old Newgate prison at Old Bailey, or even Mayfair. Instead, shortly after her cruel murder, Ann Naylor was spoken of as the Chick Lane

Ghost, an unearthly figure in white gliding through the air near the reeking gulley-hole. Now, at least, mothers who were worried about their children staying out after dark in that crime-ridden area had an effective deterrent. But the building of the terminus of the Metropolitan Railway a century later must have disturbed Ann's original spiritual roost, for the voiceless white wraith of Chick Lane metamorphosed into the Screaming Spectre of Farringdon. Even to this day people claim to hear the blood-curdling screams of a young girl echoing through the tunnels. You can readily imagine this story taking hold in the middle of the nineteenth century, when the underground was still a new phenomenon. The endless tunnels, the disturbing proximity of strangers, the noise of engines, the smell of smoke and steam — these were just the conditions in which a ghost might arise.

Purists complain that Farringdon Station is almost a hundred yards from where Ann was unceremoniously disposed of in the gulley in Chick Lane. But the current station does not share the site of the 1863 terminus, which was only ever meant to stand for as long as the railway was under development. Access was via West Street, and West Street just happened to be the new name for Chick Lane. In any case, Ann Naylor is thought to be a peripatetic spirit who also haunts Bruton Street as a girl standing at a window, though not necessarily the window of the haberdasher's shop, the whereabouts of which has never been discovered. Then again, it may be that Ann concentrates her screaming energies on Farringdon, leaving the haunting of Mayfair to her sister Mary, who was so casually murdered for her silence and so often forgotten in this tale of senseless depravity. No site has ever been proposed for the disposal of Mary's little corpse, and the body parts found in Chick Lane, which were washed by some poor souls at the local workhouse and reassembled like a ghastly jigsaw, were not enough to account for two dead girls.

And the ghost who never was? Perhaps the time has come to add another sad figure to the tradition of the London ghost. For in 1763, a year after the Metyards were hanged, Richard Rooker, who had been Sarah's lodger and Sally's kind master — or elderly lover — was found dead near Ealing Common. He had committed suicide near the Green Man tavern by cutting his throat and wrists. Haunted by this awful story, as indeed we all are as well, he might haunt Ealing yet.

You Must Not Bury Me Alive

IN THE YEAR 1788 in a house in Lambeth a man by the name of Grimaldi, aged about seventy-five, breathed his last. At his side was his daughter, Margaret. She wept, as daughters do, and then, her weeping done, she sent for a surgeon. When the surgeon arrived, Margaret spoke to him briefly. On hearing her request the medical man stepped back in horror and turned to leave. However, Margaret persisted and persuaded the surgeon to stay. He opened the bag in which he kept his various instruments. Then with a shaky hand he slowly took out a saw.

Old Grimaldi lay motionless on the bed. The waxen pallor of death gave his features a ghostly appearance. He was stretched out on the sheet as if in sleep, and in a sense he was asleep and would be for all eternity. Margaret stood over him and gave him a long look, the look, you might have thought, of a daughter who was distraught at the passing of her father. You might also have thought that it was the look of a person searching for some small sign of life — the barely perceptible rising of the chest, the infinitesimal quivering of a finger, the momentary flutter of an eyelid.

But Margaret saw no such sign. At last, turning to the surgeon, she gave him permission to continue. The surgeon stepped up to the body, steadying himself for the act he was about to perform. The blade of his saw glinted in the light of the candle Margaret held in her hand. He was ready. He pulled the shirt of the dead man down away from his throat, and then, with the rapid movements that were the hallmark of his trade, he sawed down through skin and bone until the head came clean away from the body.

And so who was this Grimaldi who went to his grave in two separate pieces? His full name was Giuseppe Grimaldi. He was a native of Genoa, and he came to London in about 1760, where he was engaged by the illustrious David Garrick to perform as a dancer and pantomime buffoon at the Theatre Royal in Drury Lane.

He may not be exactly famous — to us — but his son Joseph certainly is. For Joseph Grimaldi was the Regency actor who achieved immortality as the great pantomime clown, the original 'Joey' of circus tradition. As stars of the stage go, Joseph has outshone Giuseppe, but Giuseppe is still the star of the remarkable story that now follows.

First, as with all theatrical stories, the scene must be set. Mention has already been made of Lambeth on the south side of the River Thames, and it is in that direction that we need to bend our steps. And in particular we need to bend them in the direction of Lambeth Marsh, which is just about as evocative a name from the capital's murky past as you are ever likely to hear.

On a map of the area with the date 1767 Lambeth Marsh is an extensive tract of largely uninhabited land. These days it is the site of St Thomas's Hospital, which moved to Lambeth from Southwark in the 1870s, but in the eighteenth century the most prominent building was Lambeth Palace to the south. The thought of this considerable expanse is not particularly appealing, and the 'marsh' element of its name, which conjures images of sucking bogs and impenetrable mists, adds another layer of desolate gloominess. These are places that haunt the imagination with the weird cries of birds and the sickly smell of disease and decay. Even so, a line of dwellings can be seen on the map along a road called Stangate, and it was here that the Genoese buffoon purchased a house and garden.

The story goes that Grimaldi moved into the property in the middle of a harsh winter. The wind whistled forlornly across the marsh, its eerie sound rising at times to a howl. With the temperature plummeting the pools of water froze and snow fell, covering everything as far as the eye could see. There was no end to the cold days, no end to the freezing nights. And yet Grimaldi was not content simply to sit it out: he wanted to see what his new garden would look like in spring. He immediately had the ground planted with artificial flowers and the trees with artificial foliage and fruit. Spring, at least in his part of Lambeth, had arrived.

Now, it appears that Grimaldi's grumblings about the miseries of winter were entirely in character, and it was widely reported that he was a man of pronounced moods. These moods, which shifted with alarming ease, made him queer company. He was afraid of the fourteenth day of the month, for example, so much so that in the days leading up to the dreaded date he was prone to fits of anxiety. After the fourteenth had passed and the fifteenth had arrived, Grimaldi was a new man, cheerful and optimistic where on the previous day he had been withdrawn and morose. 'Ah!' he would declare to anyone who would listen. 'Now I am safe for another month.' The root of his superstition may have had something to do with the fact that he had not only been born on the fourteenth of one month but christened on the fourteenth of another. Oddly, he chose to be married on a fourteenth. And strangely — for in this case he had no choice in the matter — he died on another fourteenth. He also once had a dream in which the devil warned him that he was going to get him, and that he would get him on the first Friday. By 'the first Friday' the devil meant the first Friday of the month, only he refused to specify which month he had in mind. Consequently Grimaldi spent every first Friday in the company of friends, who sat up with him as a defence against the devil until the clock struck twelve, whereupon Friday gave way to Saturday and the danger passed.

More often than not, though, his mood settled into a stubborn sullenness. For hours on end he would wander round churchyards, and, if not churchyards, then burial grounds. In these mournful places, in the demesne of the dead, he would lie down and meditate, if, that is, he could find a patch of grass dry enough to afford him a degree of comfort. When not meditating he would circulate among the headstones, reading the inscriptions and trying to recreate imaginatively the circumstances in which the occupants of the graves had died, what they had died of, and how they had conducted themselves in their final moments. He was spotted once in the burial ground of St Clement Danes in Portugal Street, staring at the grave of Josias 'Joe' Miller, a comic actor and singer who had died in the 1730s. He was said to be deep in thought, although there is no record of what was or even what might have been passing through his mind. He could not have chosen a place better suited to his sombre introspections, for the Portugal Street burial ground, which was known as the Green Ground, was dangerously overcrowded. Here gravediggers fell ill and local residents were tormented by the stench.

To the east of Lambeth Marsh lay St George's Fields, which were famous not only as the assembly point for the anti-Catholic Gordon Riots of 1780, but also as the place where in 1711 a Mr Shanks staged a grinning contest, for which admission was sixpence and the prize a gold-laced hat. Giuseppe would often walk through the Fields with a bookseller friend. Unfortunately the bookseller's name has not come to light, but it is a fair guess that he had antiquarian tastes, for it is said that he and his companion would discuss 'all the superstitious legends of Germany and Great Britain'. These walks across the dreary Fields, where travelling showmen parked their caravans and the criminal classes swilled beer in the Dog and Duck, cannot have done much to lift the spirits of the saturnine Grimaldi. He was once persuaded by another friend to meet some drinking companions in a tavern in St James's Market, which was across the river in Piccadilly, but he found their jollity less than helpful. Sinking even deeper into the slough of despond, he eventually gave up trying to join in and beat a hasty retreat.

However, none of this eccentric behaviour compares with what happened when the bookseller lent the melancholy Italian a copy of *The Uncertainty of the Signs of Death*. This treatise, remarkable for its alarming title, dealt with the difficulties in determining when life had expired and the awful consequences of getting such a diagnosis wrong. Not surprisingly, it tipped Giuseppe Grimaldi over the edge. There and then he developed a morbid fear of being buried alive, and this fear drove him to a course of action which, while it almost beggars belief, is fully attested in his will.

There he made the usual provision for four of his children, among them Joseph and a daughter, Margaret. But he also made a special request to Margaret 'to see me out into my coffin and the day that I am buried to sever my head from my body, the only favour I request, and then to follow me to the place of my burial'. Only in this way could he be sure that he would be truly dead when he came to be buried, only in this way reassured that, if by some ghastly mischance he had fallen into a deathlike sleep, he would not wake to the sound of nails being driven into the lid of his coffin, or to the thump of soil being shovelled into the deep grave in which he had been deposited. And in order to ensure that Margaret carried out his grisly request, he offered her a financial incentive, one element of which — a gold watch — was alone worth seventy guineas.

The comedian Jacob de Castro noted in his memoirs that Margaret did indeed see to her father's post mortem decapitation, and, if you wish to remind yourself of the details, then feel free to read the opening paragraphs of this story again. De Castro actually made short shrift of the whole business, simply stating that Margaret, unable to perform the act herself, sent for a surgeon 'who took it' — the head — 'off'. However, anxious to lay claim to the bequest, she did the legal minimum by 'touching the instrument' — the surgeon's saw — while the operation to remove her father's head from the body to which it had for so long been attached was being performed. Not many daughters could make such a proud boast.

One wonders what life with such a father must have been like. In fact we have a pretty good idea, for Joseph's memoirs, edited by Charles Dickens, were published shortly after his own death in 1837. Giuseppe, it would seem, was a cruel father. He put Joseph on the stage at Sadler's Wells as a juvenile tumbler when he was just over two years old. A tough disciplinarian, he handed out thrashings to any of his many children — he fathered at least ten with three different women — who stepped out of line. Once, hoping to find out if he was loved or not, he feigned death by lying under a sheet in a darkened room. The irony! One of the boys, John, having whooped with delight, received a sound thrashing from his father, who had leapt up from his death-bed in a lather of rage. Joseph had said the right thing — 'Oh, what would I give to see him alive again!' — but he was so frightened by his father's anger that he hid in the coal cellar for four hours.

But what are we to say of the nightmare, which so haunted Giuseppe Grimaldi, of being buried alive? What of his taphophobia? Presumably he had suffered these products of a morbid and overactive imagination long before he read *The Uncertainty of the Signs of Death*, but it was undoubtedly this cheerless volume that gave his fear a fully defined shape. The author was an anatomist by the name of Jacques-Bénigne Winslow, who was born in Denmark but became a naturalised Frenchman, and who is remembered to science as the first person to describe the omental foramen, which is a hole of sorts lying somewhere between the stomach and the liver. In the hope of inducing the greatest possible alarm in his readers, Winslow included in his treatise a number of accounts of cases of premature burial. Some of these were decidedly bizarre, a fine example being that of an unscrupulous servant who opened his mistress's coffin to cut off the finger on which she wore a valuable ring, only to find that the pain inflicted by his knife revived the dead woman, who had never really died in the first place, or at least not in the fullest sense of the word. You may also be interested to learn that this highly improbable event took place in a churchyard in Orléans, and that the woman, having put the wretched servant to flight with her terrifying shrieks, promptly hopped out of her coffin and returned to her husband, with whom she lived for another ten years.

The classic literary realisation of old Grimaldi's disturbing vision is the story 'The Premature Burial' by Edgar Allan Poe, which was published in a Philadelphia newspaper in 1844. But this sub-genre of spine-chilling writing was not limited to creative fiction, and in 1866 *The Lancet* offered the following pen sketch of a scenario that would surely fill the boldest heart with icy terror:

The last footfall departs from the solitary churchyard, leaving the entranced sleeper behind in his hideous shell, soon to awaken to a consciousness and to a benumbed half-suffocated existence for a few minutes; or else, more horrible still, there he lies beneath the ground conscious of what has been and still is, until, by some fearful agonised struggle of the inner man at the weird phantasmagoria which has passed across his mental vision, he awakes to a bodily vivification as desperate in its torment for a brief period as has been that of his physical activity. But it is soon past. There is scarcely room to turn over in the wooden chamber; and what can avail a few shrieks and struggles of a half-stifled, cramped-up man!

But the final word on the subject of premature burial and its prevention was a book published in 1896 by William Tebb and Edward Perry Vollum, in which a surprising number of historical figures featured. And there the subject must be laid to rest, as it were, but not before mentioning that, if we are to believe Tebb and Vollum, the philosopher George Berkeley, the Irish politician Daniel O'Connell and the statesman and poet Lord Lytton all suffered from the same mental torment as Grimaldi. The novelist Wilkie Collins would leave a message on his dressing-table asking to be very carefully examined if found 'dead' in the morning, and Hans Christian Andersen carried in his pocket a note to the same effect. Old Giuseppe, it would seem, was in very good company.

The Witch of Moorgate

HAD YOU CHANCED to find yourself in Moor Lane in the late summer of 1821, in the reign of George IV, you would almost certainly have been looking nervously over your shoulder. For Moor Lane, near London Wall, was a narrow and dingy thoroughfare hemmed in by mean dwellings. On both sides there were dark and menacing passages, and one of these opened out into New Court, where you might well have encountered an old woman kneeling on the hard cobblestones in full view of one and all, and raining down curses on her enemies. She was Mary — or 'Mammy' — Calder. And she was believed by many to be a witch.

Mammy Calder was not the first of her kind. Far from it. For a very long time witches had been a reason why fearful Londoners, and not only those Londoners living in New Court in Moor Lane, might lie awake at night. Take the case of Elizabeth Sawyer of Edmonton. She cut a frightening figure, for she was afflicted with a stoop and had only one eye. Local children claimed that they had seen her feeding two white ferrets with bread and milk, which was taken as a sure sign of her maleficence, for it was believed that one of these creatures, which had been observed in the thatch over her house, was an evil spirit, or a devil, in disguise. When Elizabeth was put on trial at the Old Bailey in 1621, charged with murdering three of her neighbours, she was found to have a teat, which was the mark of a witch, growing near her anus. By her own admission she was devoted to Satan, who visited her three times a week in the form of a dog, which was sometimes black and sometimes white, but at all times answered to the name Tom and sucked her blood through the teat. Although acquitted of two of the murders, she was found guilty of the third and hanged at Tyburn.

Consider also the case of Joan Peterson of Wapping. She too was hanged as a witch at Tyburn, but she was not entirely bad. She once cured a wretched fellow of a relentless headache — it had kept him awake for five weeks — with three draughts of a miraculous potion. She also helped a cowkeeper's wife find the woman who had cursed one of her cows, a curious procedure that involved boiling a pan of her own urine, in which the perpetrator's face was seen as if in a mirror. But Joan was better known for her wickedness. When one of her patients failed to pay her for a cure, he found himself wasting away. In the few days remaining to him he spent twelve hours raving and raging as if insane, and another twelve slobbering helplessly as if he had lost all his teeth. Joan was also reputed to have bewitched a neighbour's infant child, and she had at least two familiars. One, a squirrel, held parley with her all night long, instructing her in her evil ways. Another, a black dog, communed with her by nuzzling up against her armpits. And were these reports mere rumour? No, they were not. For there were eyewitnesses, and Joan stood no chance when she was tried at the Old Bailey in the spring of 1652.

Consider finally the case of Jinney Bingham. By some she was called Mother Damnable, by others Mother Red Cap. There were even those who knew her as the Shrew of Kentish Town, which makes it obvious where she lived. She had a large bottle nose flanked by furrowed and leathery cheeks, sunken eyes peering out from beneath shaggy black eyebrows, and a steadfast gaze. She dribbled from the corners of her mouth, which stretched from ear to ear. Her forehead was wrinkled, and all that lay above it was covered by the red cap that had earned her one of her names. Around her shoulders was a coarse woollen cloak, dark grey and striped, and mended with black patches resembling bats. As a companion she had a black cat, and over the years she had consorted with at least three men, one of whom was found crouching in her oven, burnt to a cinder. She escaped the death sentence when a witness claimed that the dead man would climb into the oven of his own accord to avoid the rough side of her tongue.

Jinney could tell fortunes and cure terrible diseases, but she was heckled by the people of Kentish Town, who would gather in crowds outside her cottage, hooting and yelling. She met her own end when the devil visited her cottage, and you must not doubt that he did so, for the crowd saw him with their own eyes. She was found the next day sitting in front of her fireplace with a teapot, and dead as dead can be. In the teapot was a potion, which was tested on her black cat, whereupon its hair fell out and it died. She herself was as stiff as a board, and the undertaker had to break her arms and legs in order to get her into a coffin.

Such was the tradition of the London witch, the examples Mammy Calder had to live up to, or down to, depending on how you look at it. Mammy was an elderly widow. She rented out the first and second floors of her house in New Court, keeping the ground floor for her own use and supplementing her income by taking in washing. Her lodgers on the first floor were a Mrs Walcot and her attractive and lively young daughter, Miss Walcot. The Walcots were close friends of Mrs Dale, who lived on the second floor with her husband. Mr Dale was a nervous man, not only because he owed the landlady ten weeks' rent, but also because the old lady had threatened to 'set God's curse on him' if he did not pay up immediately. He was trying to cheat a helpless widow, she said. And by all accounts her torrent of abuse and menacing tone seriously rattled Mr Dale.

Mammy may have been a widow, but she certainly was not helpless, and she was able to exploit her terrifying reputation to get her own way. Although New Court was in a modern metropolis, its residents suspected that they had a witch in their midst. Life for them was hard and brutal, liable to setbacks and reverses, and full of misfortunes of precisely the sort Mammy prayed for in her very public performances in the middle of the courtyard. She was merciless in her persecution of those who crossed her, and we learn from newspaper reports that the thrust of her devilish invocations, which she uttered 'in the most solemn and fervent manner', was 'that their food might not nourish them, that their cats might not mew, nor their trees grow'. She might have added further details, but the general intention was clear, namely that her enemies suffer horribly. And to the impoverished residents of Moor Lane, and Sugar Loaf Court, and Ram's Head Court, and Seven Star Court, and Vine Court, it must have appeared that Mammy's curses did indeed come true.

In some respects Mammy did not play the game. She did not affect a repulsive appearance. She did not stoop like Elizabeth Sawyer or dribble like Jinney Bingham. She did not have familiars, or, if she did, no one ever mentioned them. She did not brew potions, as Joan Peterson did, and she most assuredly did not boil urine in a pan. On the other hand, she had a good line in fortune telling, and there was a constant stream of neighbours, mainly young women, coming to her bedroom to have their cards read and their futures told. Of course, it was not hard to tell what the future held in store for a young woman living in a squalid court in the London of the 1820s. The best employment she could hope for was domestic service. Even marriage was unlikely to be all she hoped for, bringing with it one pregnancy after another and with each pregnancy the danger of death from puerperal fever. And bringing up a large family in a cramped and unhygienic slum dwelling was a recipe for a life of endless hardship.

Entertaining these unfortunate young women from her bed, Mammy turned over the yellowing cards with her bony fingers. Her unhappy, downtrodden clients hankered after a prosperity they would never enjoy and yearned for a happiness they would never achieve, and they were all too willing to pin their hopes on the haughty stare of a king or a queen, the grinning smirk of a jack, the meaningless patterns of red diamonds and hearts and black spades and clubs. And so on hearing that they were sure to meet a handsome dark-haired stranger — king of clubs — or that they would have a change of fortune for the better — ten of diamonds — or that they might make a wealthy marriage — nine of clubs — or that they should take care to avoid a jealous stranger — jack of spades — they eagerly gave Mammy the payment she deserved and demanded. While some handed her ready cash, others paid in kind by doing her lucrative washing and ironing for her.

However, it would seem that Mammy Calder had not read her own cards when she complained to Mr Dale, who lived on the second floor, not only that he owed her money, but also that his wife had been rude to her. As it happened, Mr Dale was genuinely scared of Mammy, and the newspapers observed that he was completely unmanned by

the solemnity of manner and voice she had assumed, aided by the practised movements of a countenance that could express all the terrific contortions of the Sybil.

The Sybil was the frenzied oracular priestess of the ancient world, but Mrs Dale was not so easily taken in. She showed defiance in the face of Mammy's threats, which was too much for her husband, who gave her a fearful beating in the hope that this might placate the object of his fear.

The matter went from bad to worse. Mrs Dale blamed Mammy for the lamming she had received at her husband's hands. Wanting revenge, she decided to enlist the help of Mrs and Miss Walcot, her two cronies on the floor below. The first step was to fashion a model of a witch by dressing up a doll with a long pointed hat. The doll was also made to carry a birchwood broom in one hand and a pack of cards in the other. The final effect was a miniature version of Mammy Calder. The role of the Walcots was to allow Mrs Dale to hang the doll from the second floor by a string, so that it dangled in front of their window. As their window was on the first floor, the effigy was low enough to be visible from the street or the court, and it is likely that the neighbours enjoyed a discreet laugh at Mammy's expense. Of course, the one person who would not have laughed, other than Mammy herself, was Mrs Dale's twitchy husband. However, to avoid another scene, Mrs Dale had waited for him to be out of the house before commencing operations.

Mammy was not to be insulted, and demanded that the doll be taken down immediately. But the triumvirate of Mrs Dale and Mrs and Miss Walcot only laughed at this feeble attempt at intimidation. When Mammy scuttled up to the first-floor room, her tormentors stood in her way. However, she was not ready to admit defeat. She might be old but she was strong, thanks either to her supernatural powers or to her incessant laundering. Fighting through the ranks of the enemy and breaking into the room, she reached through the window to retrieve the doll. And retrieve the doll she did, but not before Miss Walcot, with youth and pluck on her side, stepped forward to confront her. The witch gave the girl a wallop. She then attacked her with flailing fists and unpleasantly sharp fingernails. Finally she grabbed Miss Walcot's lovely long hair, pulling her from one side of the room to the other. What Mrs Walcot and Mrs Dale were doing while all this was going on is not recorded.

Mammy's victory did not last long. She was summoned to appear before Alderman Christopher Smith at the Guildhall on a charge of violent assault against the person of Miss Walcot. The story was told, and the sprightly lass was examined for signs of physical violence. None could be found. Well, almost none, for she had in fact suffered a little scratch, which could only be seen by the court when she uncovered her shoulder. The newspapers offered the inconsequential comment that it was a very pretty white shoulder.

Mammy denied being a conjuror or a witch or a fortune teller. She insisted that she earned her living by washing and ironing — when, that is, she was feeling well enough or strong enough to get out of bed — and that only the week before Mrs Walcot had paid seven shillings for her services. Mrs Walcot remarked tartly that the old woman earned more by telling fortunes in bed than by honest labour. But Mammy's response to this outrageous accusation was to point out that she was not in any way *avoiding* doing her work. She was simply *freed* from doing her work by neighbours who were grateful to her for giving them a glimpse of the future. But in the end her greatest asset was not the power of her arguments but the enlightened attitudes of the times. Being feisty and outspoken as well as unmarried and unattractive no longer meant that an old woman was a witch. In any other age Mammy would have suffered the same fate — the scaffold — as the Witches of Edmonton and Wapping. Or she would have been found dead in her cottage, like the Shrew of Kentish Town, reviled and ridiculed by one and all.

If Miss Walcot expected reparation for the alleged assault on her person, none was forthcoming. Alderman Smith was evidently less susceptible to her charms than the newspaper reporter who admired that pretty white shoulder of hers. He — the Alderman — decided that Mammy must pay the costs of the summons and the hearing. Anyone else would have been delighted at the outcome, for the case was then dismissed, but Mammy was furious at what she regarded as an injustice. She announced that she did not have the money to pay the costs, and that even if she had she would not pay them. She would suffer any imprisonment — she would 'go to all the prisons in the world' — before they got anything out of her. With a sigh Alderman Smith ordered her to be detained until the money was paid. Even then Mammy did not go quietly, and it was reported that

when put into the lock-up room at the office, her fit of Sibylline fury came on; she threatened vengeance upon poor Herdsfield, the officer who had locked her up, and knelt down on the floor to pray God's curse upon him.

Officer Herdsfield, who was a sensible fellow, merely laughed, which made Mammy bluster and blather all the more. She was a witch, more or less, to the very end.

The Ghosts of Berkeley Square

THE STORY GOES that a young girl, whose name, sadly, has disappeared, once had a terrifying encounter of a supernatural kind in one of Mayfair's grander houses. Given that the story is more legend than chronicle, it is infuriatingly short on details, which at least leaves plenty of scope for nervous imaginations. But here is the outline. The girl found herself in one of the rooms of the house, where she experienced things so horrifying that when she finally emerged she was seen to be completely deranged. Fear — fear of whom or what? — had driven her mad. Unfortunately the nature and extent of the horror remained locked in the deepest and least accessible corners of the poor girl's mind, for she had so lost the ability to speak coherently that she was unable to say what it was she had seen, or heard, or felt in that ghastly chamber.

Mayfair would probably strike most people as a safe and thoroughly salubrious area. On its borders lie the lovely open spaces of Hyde Park and Green Park, the shopper's paradise that is Oxford Street, and the broad and noble avenue that is Piccadilly. No, you do not easily think of Mayfair as a place of hauntings, or of strange atmospheres, or of voices from the grave. In this most fashionable part of the capital you do not expect to be tapped on the shoulder in an empty street at night, to turn to see who did the tapping, and to see no one at all.

Well, the wretched girl who went insane knew differently, if, that is, she knew anything after her terrifying ordeal. Not that the horror of hauntings in Mayfair ends with her, for there have been many mournful sightings of lost souls. A ghostly child dressed in a kilt and seen at a top floor window, supposedly killed by her nurse, is one. A curious white or brown mist — all that was left of a young woman who jumped to her death from a window, again on a top floor, to escape the clutches of a lecherous uncle — is another. Then there is the young man whose ravings had him confined to an attic, and the two sailors surprised by a white-faced man with a gaping mouth — or was it just some sort of shapeless mass? — one of whom fell to his death on the railings outside the house. And so on.

What these stories have in common is that the grisly incidents they describe all happened in the same place. The attic and the window and the rooms and the railings were those of one and the same house. And that house is at 50 Berkeley Square, almost exactly in the centre of Mayfair.

This elegant townhouse on the west side of a garden square certainly does not look from the outside as if it would be especially troubled by melancholy mists and ghosts in kilts. No doubt the unwholesome reputation it enjoyed at one time had a lot to do with the popularity of stories about haunted houses in nineteenth-century newspapers, and the huge crowds that gathered outside on the pavement, waiting to see if one of its many ghosts would appear, must have been routinely disappointed. This, of course, is not to say that there never have been ghosts or hauntings in the house in Berkeley Square. But the fact is that none of the reports of apparitions — of graveyard gibberings and scuttling footsteps — is even remotely trustworthy. Few claimants would have had reason, let alone permission, to set foot inside the house.

No part of the long story of no. 50 seems to be true, *except* for the part concerning one occupant, the reclusive and eccentric Thomas Myers.

Who was Thomas Myers? He was the son of another Thomas Myers, an enterprising fellow who sailed to India at the tender age of seventeen to join the East India Company, and went on to become Accomptant-General in Bengal. By the time Myers senior was thirty-six he had made his fortune. Returning to England, he was elected Member of Parliament for Harwich and married the eighteen-year-old daughter of an aristocratic family at Wyke House in Isleworth, which later gained fame, or infamy, as a mental asylum. Myers's young wife, Mary, only lived to be twenty-four. However, by the time she died she had given birth to two children, of whom the older was the Thomas of our Berkeley Square tale. The younger was a girl called Mary, who was named after her mother. Thomas was born in 1803 and Mary in 1804. Both were baptised in St George's Church in Hanover Square.

The children's father never remarried after the death of his wife. From 1810 to 1812 he served as Member of Parliament in a second constituency — Yarmouth on the Isle of Wight — after which he retired from public life.

From this point on there is little information about him other than that he owned a house in Tilney Street in Mayfair and a property, Greys Hall, in Sible Hedingham in Essex. A bit more is known about his death, though. First, he died in 1835 at the age of seventy-one. Then, in keeping with his taste in high-end accommodation, he had himself laid to rest in the cemetery in Kensal Green. This famous place of burial had only been open for two years. A fine illustration that appeared in *The Mirror of Literature, Amusement, and Instruction* only a few years later in 1838 made it plain that it was already *the* place to be buried. With its grand Anglican chapel — all classical columns, like a Roman temple — it conferred on its residents an air of sturdy permanence.

Maybe so, but on murky and misty days, when the imagination might well run riot, Kensal Green would have taken on a very different aspect. To mourners and strollers alike the grand monuments and mausoleums would have seemed austere and oppressive, the lesser tombs mean and inadequate. The mortal remains of the dead would have seemed to lie behind only inches of stone or beneath only inches of soil, ready to rise at the slightest provocation and flit mournfully along the cemetery's winding paths. And at night the shadows and the fitful and sickly gleam of a yellow moon would have instilled thrilling fear and deep unease in equal measure.

At his death the old man left Thomas and his sister Mary very wealthy. They were now in their thirties and unmarried, which in view of their society connections is surprising. Mary continued to live in what had been the family house in Tilney Street with two or three servants. Her living arrangements appear quite modest when compared with those of her neighbours, Mr and Mrs Reginald Brett and their one-month-old son, who had *nine* live-in servants to care for them. As for Thomas …

Thomas Myers is even more of a cipher than his sister. He appears in the 1851 census as an annuitant, aged forty-six and lodging in Mayfair at 4 Chapel Street West, which is now Aldford Street, in a house owned by a certain Ann Williams. There is no evidence that he paid land tax in London at any time from 1835 until about 1859, which he would have done if he had owned or leased a property. Either he took lodgings or he lived outside the capital. Then again, a relative by marriage, Lady Dorothy Nevill, described him as 'exceedingly eccentric', adding rather unkindly that he exhibited his idiosyncratic tendencies 'to a degree that bordered on lunacy', which suggests that he may have been privately institutionalised.

At this stage 50 Berkeley Square had yet to acquire its notoriety. For many years it had been occupied by the Honourable Elizabeth Curzon, who died aged ninety-one in April 1859, whereupon Thomas Myers moved in. He remained there until his death in November 1874. His odd habits certainly contributed to rumours of hauntings.

For example, it was said that he had not ventured out of doors for some twenty years. He slept by day, and, to make matters worse, he wandered through the house by night, supposedly dematerialising in one room and then rematerializing in the next with all the incorporeal insouciance of a ghost. In fact he was thought of locally as being exactly that — a ghost — and it was reported that his nocturnal flitting was accompanied by weird noises that seemed to rise up from some deep place inside his skeletal sound-box. Occasionally the house was lit at dead of night, which must have suggested to the suitably curious and inquisitive neighbours scenes of unspeakable ghastliness.

To those passing along the street during the day the house had a sombre mien, the sight of which induced depressing thoughts and a general lowering of the spirits. The windows were black with antique dust, which only strengthened the impression that the house was empty of human content. Certainly no owner was ever seen leaving the premises, as most house owners generally do on occasions, stepping on to the pavement with a friendly nod to the passers-by, and staring up at the sky to decide on the need for an umbrella before it is too late. And so it was all the more baffling to those with an interest in no. 50 that deliveries of essentials — coal, for example, and provisions — were made from time to time. The deliveries were taken by a servant, who would have been a valuable source of inside information if he had ever agreed to answer anyone's questions. But this lugubrious flunky remained, appropriately, as silent as the grave.

The state of the house must have been a constant source of annoyance to Thomas's illustrious neighbours. What is more, he had long ago ceased paying his taxes, so much so that in 1873, that is to say the year before his death, the tax collector for the parish of St George Hanover Square, whose name was Knox, was forced to apply to the magistrates for a warrant of distress against his goods. Thomas was not exactly poor, but he was rather individual in his habits, a point made by a newspaper report on the Berkeley Square hauntings.

On his decease he left his sister the lease on a house that was dirty and neglected. Her home in Tilney Street was comfortable enough, and 50 Berkeley Square stood empty until 1884, when the lease ran out and the house was bought by Lord and Lady Selkirk. All this time interest in the supernatural goings-on had continued to grow. In 1876 a newspaper article claimed that the London Association of Spiritualists wanted to exorcise the ghost that had supposedly haunted the house for fifty years, though there is no evidence that they carried out this drastic plan.

Stories about Thomas also began to surface. In one of these he had leased and furnished the house over fifty years previously in order to prepare for a marriage that never took place. Only days before the ceremony his unfeeling — and unnamed — fiancée jilted him. Then he became a recluse who lived with 'two or three crusty servants'. According to this account of Thomas he was nothing so much as a male counterpart of Miss Havisham. For all the world he might have been living in a state of loveless suspended animation, half-dressed for the altar, a skin-and-bones version of his younger self. His life had ended, and every clock in the house had stopped ticking at the moment of his betrayal.

However, the story cannot be correct, for Thomas only lived in the house for fifteen years, which is way off the fifty years he is supposed to have spent sorrowing over his shattered dreams of marriage. Possibly he had moved there in 1859, fifteen years before his death, intending or hoping to be married at some point. After all, there is no reason why a man in his fifties should not marry. Somehow, though, this does not sound like Thomas. If anything, he was jilted as a young man, when his eccentricities began to express themselves. But there is not a jot of evidence to support such a theory.

This is not to say that the tales of an empty house are entirely without foundation, and it is a strange fact that Thomas is absent from the 1861 and 1871 censuses. In each case the sole entry for 50 Berkeley Square is a middle-aged servant from Darlington in Yorkshire by the name of Eleanor or Ellen Porter. Could it be that at the time of the censuses the reclusive Thomas was in the house but did not want to declare himself? Maybe it suited him that people thought that the house was haunted. That would at least have been one way of getting others to leave him alone.

What is particularly interesting is that hauntings and generally unpleasant events 'belonging' to other places in this part of London came to be associated with no. 50. Thanks to fictional stories in the newspapers and a popular novel set in Berkeley Square, which many readers were convinced was based on fact, this once run-down building gained a reputation that has persisted to the present day. It even appears as a venue for a Charles Dickens Ghost Club Mission in the *Assassin's Creed Syndicate* video game! Ironically, the loudest voice denouncing these stories came from within the house itself. The house agent sent by Thomas's sister to inspect the premises after his death found himself face to face with two servants, one of whom may well have been the woman from Darlington. 'Well, is it true,' he asked them, 'that strange things happen here and odd noises can be heard?' 'No.' 'Do you *never* see ghosts?' the house agent then asked, at which the two women burst out laughing. 'We never see'd none!'

If anything in the saga is haunting — pun very much intended — it is not the rumours of ghosts and ghouls but the sad lives of Thomas and Mary Myers. Neither married. Mary never had children, and, even though she left a hundred and sixty-nine thousand pounds in her will, she had passed her life in joyless frugality. Thomas suffered a degree of self-neglect that would now be recognised as a mental health condition. Indeed, the only recognition his condition received was in the form of half-baked tales of a haunted house — of *the* haunted house — the Haunted House at 50 Berkeley Square.

The Ghost of Lizzie Church

LONDON HOSPITALS ARE peculiarly susceptible to the supernatural, it would seem. For example, the Royal National Orthopaedic Hospital in Stanmore is haunted by a nun. Guy's Hospital, hard by London Bridge Station, also has a resident spectre, a ghostly nurse who makes a nuisance of herself by clattering up and down the wards with noisy footsteps. More macabre even than these apparitions is the grey lady who haunts St Thomas's Hospital in Lambeth. Rumour has it that she appears at the bedsides of poor unfortunates hovering on the brink of death, although we must assume that she times her visits to give her victims long enough to tell others that she has dropped in on them. If not, we would be none the wiser. And then — then there is the case of

University College Hospital. And if you want to find out what happened at University College Hospital, read on.

Ruth Darbyshire — the hospital matron throughout the 1920s and 1930s — was roused from sleep by a piercing scream. She was awake immediately. She wondered for a second or two if she had been dreaming, if her mind had simply convinced itself that what it was hearing was real. But the scream had been too vivid, too definite to be anything other than real. She knew that she had to investigate and so she got out of bed. The uncomfortable sensation of sleep abruptly cut short was one she was familiar with, an experience that had become almost routine in her many years as a nurse living in hospital accommodation. She was well used to disturbed nights, to sleep shattered in the small hours by unexpected noises or cries.

Ruth stepped out into the dark corridor. The rooms in this part of the hospital had been allotted to the ward maids, who at this hour were all deep in sleep. All but one: the door of one room was open. A bedside lamp was alight in the room, casting a yellow glow into the corridor. Ruth walked towards the door, where she saw a figure standing outside the room, half hidden in the shadows. The figure was that of a young woman. She was looking away from Ruth, her gaze fixed on the far end of the corridor, where it disappeared into deep darkness. When Ruth approached, the other woman was so shocked that she let out another scream. Her expression was one of terror: her features were taut, her eyes wide, her mouth half open. Her hands were clutched tightly together, but her arms and shoulders were trembling with fear.

However, when she realised that it was Ruth there in the corridor with her, the young maid seemed to be reassured. She was new to the hospital, the most recent recruit on the ward. After a while she was calm enough to speak. Having gathered her thoughts, but still with a look of anxiety in her eyes, she began to explain why she had been screaming. She had seen the ghost, she said. *The* ghost. The ghost of Nurse Lizzie Church — the Lizzie Church who, as everyone was well aware, haunted University College Hospital. She had been told about the ghost, she went on. The moment she arrived the other maids told her about it. They would not stop going on about the ghost — on and on *and on*. Ruth was dismayed. She asked her what tales she had heard, what the others had said that had so frightened her. They were horrible tales, the girl replied. Horrible, horrible tales.

About a nurse who had worked at the hospital once but was now dead. She was murdered, and her body was thrown out of a window. The window was so near, so near. Right by the rooms where the maids slept.

Ruth briskly told the girl that there had been no such murder. And there had certainly not been a dead body tumbling out of a window. Then, having sent her back to bed, she returned to her own room and shut the door. But she was not yet ready to go back to sleep, and, having settled beneath the sheets, she fell to thinking. How ridiculous it was, she told herself, that young women in this modern era still believed in ghosts. The twentieth century had begun, signalling the end, she would have thought, of old superstitions and antiquated fears. Having said that, she had once listened to the tales herself and had wondered about them. In fact she had heard about Lizzie Church so often that she had even persuaded herself to search through the hospital records for — for what? — well, for anything out of the ordinary. Naturally there had been nothing, not even a suggestion of a murder or a suicide. The only disturbing discovery had been the story of a nurse who had been dismissed for 'walking out' with a hospital porter. That had been in 1849. Ruth could not begin to imagine what life would have been like for such a girl when she was sent away so unceremoniously without a reference ...

Here a question arises. Why are there so many tales of ghost nurses? How do we account for these curious spectres, who seem to us to manage effortlessly their two roles as carers and scarers? The reason probably has a great deal to do with our experience of being in hospital. For the painful fact of the matter is that we, the patients, do not always get better. We might get worse. We might even die. So Death lurks in hospitals. Death hides in corners — corners we hope never to turn — and it waits in operating theatres — theatres we hope never to be in. But even if we never meet Death in hospital, we may find that Death invades our thoughts. We lie alone for hour after hour with our minds wandering distractedly. At night, when we cannot sleep, we see the nurses going about their duties, moving softly and stealthily, and we hear them in the way we imagine that we would hear the shades of the dead, whispering, whispering. The lights are low, and dark shapes play on the walls. The corridors are quiet, but unsettling sounds — a cough, a moan, a brief cry of pain — come to us from afar.

Now, the story told by Miss Darbyshire, as we have seen, took place in University College Hospital. While the College itself, which was on the other side of Gower Street, was regarded as a triumph of nineteenth-century classicism, complete with pediment and Corinthian columns, Alfred Waterman's red-brick hospital, which opened its doors in 1906, was a very different affair. The building was gloomy, to say the least. Indeed, to a certain type of sensitive mind it was more than merely gloomy: it was downright creepy. And the unsettling atmosphere that always pervades a building of this description readily lent itself to tales of a ghostly nurse. Quite possibly, though, the hauntings were older than Waterman's edifice, for there were reports that Lizzie Church had been spotted in the rather less gothic hospital that originally stood on the Gower Street site.

As you would expect of a deceased member of the medical profession, Lizzie is a watchful and kindly spirit with none of the malice you associate with the ghosts that haunt graveyards, or the poltergeists that disturb houses. Patients who have been visited by her comment on the kind treatment they have received from a nurse dressed in the bluish-grey uniform of former days. Occasionally it is claimed that she only appears when morphine is being administered, and that she hovers at the side of the bed, looking attentively over the shoulder of the doctor or nurse as they perform the injection. In these cases she is regarded as the embodiment of benevolent intervention, a guarantor of the efficacy of a miraculous drug that has been used to treat conditions from delirium tremens to asthma and headaches, delivering rapid and effective relief from unendurable pain. But her spectral presence, her visits from wherever she resides in the company of the dead, are reminders of and cautions against the dangers of morphine, which brings succour, yes, but also ensnares, catching its victims in the net of an ineluctable addiction.

There is another version of the story, often told, which begins harmlessly enough with Lizzie, a trainee nurse at the time, being instructed to look after a patient who was seriously ill. But the story descends into tragedy when Lizzie went to tend him for the first time, and realised that he was her fiancé. She was dismayed, for the last time she had seen him he had been the picture of health, and they had talked happily about their future together. When he was prescribed morphine, as required by his treatment, Lizzie was left to administer the injection. But she made a mistake over the amount of the drug the poor man's condition called for, and he died, having received a fatal dose. Lizzie was distraught. Unable to accept the loss of her dear fiancé, and tormented by the thought that she had been the agent of his death, she committed suicide. Thereafter she has attended patients who have been prescribed morphine, watching the procedure closely and wearing in her spectral features a look of obsessive concern.

There would appear to have been no murders or suicides at University College Hospital that would explain the genesis of the ghost. But there was a real Lizzie Church who worked at the hospital from 1869 until 1885, when she met an untimely end reportedly caused by her professional activities. Her full name was Elizabeth Ann Church, and she was born in 1839 in Burbage, a village in Wiltshire. She had a difficult start in life, for her mother, Emma, was unmarried and very young. Up to the age of four Lizzie lived with her grandparents. Then her mother, who was working as a servant, gave birth to a second illegitimate child, a little boy who died very soon after birth. Within a few days Emma herself was dead. Possibly she had contracted puerperal fever, a common cause of postpartum fatalities.

Lizzie remained with her grandparents until she too went into service, the path so many working-class

Victorian women were obliged to follow. She was obviously competent, for by the time she was twenty she had found employment with a solicitor in Wiltshire and was working for him as a cook. At some stage between 1861 and 1869 she moved from Wiltshire to London, where she made the decision to become a nurse. Why she did this is not entirely clear. A newspaper report written at the time of her death said that she was inspired by the care she had experienced herself as a patient at University College Hospital. Whatever the truth of the matter, she began training as a probationer with the Sisters of the Order of All Saints, a religious body that not only supplied the hospital with nurses but also trained recruits.

Throughout her sixteen years at the hospital Lizzie was greatly respected as an accomplished professional. Her dedication was recognised in 1879 when she was one of the ten recipients of the newly instituted Order of St Katharine, a prestigious award named after the patron saint of nurses, St Catherine of Siena. A ceremony was held on the 7th of July in the library at University College, presided over by the Duke of Westminster and other notables. Lady Lucy Adela Jenner, who was the wife of one of the hospital's professors, made the award to

Lizzie and one of her colleagues, Ellen Harrington. They were presented with a written warrant, an armlet and a brooch with the insignia of the Order — a white oval with a green border and the monogram 'St. K' in the centre. They were also given a fifty-pound addition to their salary for the next three years. Sadly, Lizzie did not meet Miss Florence Nightingale, who was expected at the event but was too ill to attend. The doyenne of nursing sent her apologies, but it is perhaps just as well that she was not at the ceremony in person, for she did not approve of money being spent on the awards, believing that it would be better used in training nurses.

The beneficial impact of Lizzie's unstinting efforts is recognised in this extract from a Yorkshire newspaper, the *Beverley and East Riding Recorder*:

Many a poor sufferer who has lain in lingering pain in the hospital wards of London University College has blessed the kindly face and gentle hand of 'Lizzie Church', the patient and skilful nurse of the Order of St Katherine, who for years past has smoothed the pain pressed pillows of sojourners in the hall of healing in connection with our metropolitan medical college.

But her career was not to last much longer. In late 1884 she was given the responsibility of caring for a bedridden medical colleague — he was suffering from a malignant illness — but early in the following year she died. Her obituaries suggested that her death was linked with her patient's illness. In actual fact she had died of sanguineous apoplexy — what we would now call a stroke — brought on by the strain of her nursing duties. The place of her death was not University College Hospital, which is perhaps surprising, given the scene of her haunting, but the home at 36 Cavendish Square of Dr Christopher Heath, who was the Holme Professor of Clinical Surgery at University College. The doctor present at her death was Sydney Ringer, who was also a Holme Professor, not of Clinical Surgery but of Clinical Medicine.

Lizzie's colleagues were shocked at her death: she was only forty-six. A funeral service was held four days later at All Saints Church in Gordon Street — just a short walk from the hospital, and now demolished — and it was attended by Lizzie's fellow nurses and other medical colleagues. The church was crowded with admirers, and, when the service ended, she was taken to Brompton Cemetery to be laid to rest. She left a modest sum in her will — a little over a hundred and sixty pounds — which went to the Crown.

One may well wonder how the story about Lizzie Church and the morphine began. In particular, the question must be asked whether morphine played a part in her own death. Was she given the drug to ease the pain brought on by her stroke, and did that dose ultimately bring about her end? Those of a suspicious turn of mind might look at cases at the end of the nineteenth century of nurses driven to suicide, either by difficulties in their personal lives or by trouble they were having with their colleagues. There were many. So it is not unreasonable to suppose that a middle-aged woman doing a physically demanding job might indeed have taken morphine, either deliberately or accidentally. On the other hand, it might be thought unlikely that Sydney Ringer, an important and respected member of the medical profession, would perjure himself on the death certificate, even if by doing so he hoped to spare an esteemed colleague the shame of being exposed as a suicide or addict.

Nurse Elizabeth Ann Church duly entered University College Hospital mythology. So too did the details of her unhappy death. A memorial was placed in the ward where she worked in order to be seen by colleagues and new members of staff. In time her true story was forgotten, at which point the new story — the story of a ghost who haunted the night-time wards of University College Hospital — took its place.

Other books you might enjoy …

The Splintered Eye
&
Other Haunting Stories

Karen & William Ellis-Rees

From the authors of *London Ghosts Unveiled* comes this collection of chilling stories. A Victorian clergyman is tormented from beyond the grave. A lonely photographer struggles to separate image from reality in post-war London. A terrifying journey down the Regent's Canal turns a young man's world upside down for good. A child's innocence is shattered at Christmas.

The eleven disturbing tales in *The Splintered Eye* reveal how greed, cruelty and violence bind the spirits of the dead to the world of the living.

The Elephant of Exeter Change

A Tale of Cruelty and Confinement in Georgian London

William Ellis-Rees

This is the remarkable true story of one of the most notorious incidents in early nineteenth-century London. A five-ton elephant confined in a menagerie above a shopping arcade in the Strand suddenly goes berserk, with horrifying and tragic consequences.

Set against a backdrop of theatres, schools of anatomy and dangerous slums, the story offers a vivid insight into life in the rougher quarters of the city. The showmen and the animal dealers who operate in this shadowy world are roguish impresarios masquerading as respectable scientists. But at the heart of the story are two good men: a ship's captain and the founder of the new Zoological Society of London.

Printed in Great Britain
by Amazon

47366242R00081